THINGS COMMON, PROPERLY

PETER WHIGHAM

Things Common, Properly

SELECTED POEMS 1942—1982

BLACK SWAN BOOKS

First edition

Published by
BLACK SWAN BOOKS Ltd.
P.O. Box 327
Redding Ridge, CT 06876
ISBN 0–933806–21–3

Printed in Hungary by Szegedi Nyomda

for

FRANCES WHIGHAM

who has lived the occasions
of so many of these poems

'Tis hard, to speake things common, properly.

BEN JONSON
Horace's *Art of Poetry*

ACKNOWLEDGEMENTS

These are all the poems written between 1942 and 1982 the author wants to keep in print. *The Poems of Catullus* (1966), *The Poems of Meleager* (with Peter Jay, 1975) and the versions from Martial collected in *Letter to Juvenal* (1984) have been excluded from the selection. There are two exceptions: 'Codex Veronensis', which forms the epigraph to *The Poems of Catullus,* and 'Priapus' which, though certainly spurious, was included as Carmen XVIII. Acknowledgements for these, therefore, to Penguin Books and to California University Press. Many of the poems originally formed part of other collections; I am therefore grateful to Neville Spearman, Sand Dollar Press, and The Press of the Pegacycle Lady, publishers respectively of *Clear Lake Comes from Enjoyment* (with Denis Goacher, 1959), *The Crystal Mountain* (1970) and *Langue d'Oeil* (1971). Others, notably the long adaptation from Semonides of Amorgos, 'The Genealogy of Women', and the collection of poems about childhood, *The Feast & The Gypsies,* are published here for the first time. For the rest, files and memory over forty years are speckled with *lacunae.* Any list would certainly include three anthologies: *23 Modern British Poets* (ed. John Matthias), *The Greek Anthology* (ed. Peter Jay), and *20 Times in One Place*; and such publications as *Agenda, Arion* (1st series), *Artisan, The European, New Measure, Shenandoah, Spectrum, Voyages, The Western Mail, The Worth Record,* as well (of course) as the Third Programme of the B.B.C. ...

P.W.

CONTENTS

Poems 1942—1962

THE QUESTERS

How fade the glories of forgotten days
　　Within these castle walls! The lives of old
　　In fadeless drifts of crimsons, browns & gold
Piled high against the iron stone make blaze
With constant memories the autumnal haze,
　　That still for us the antique tale be told
　　Of times when o'er the sloping hills there rolled
The distant horn that sounded lost forays.

Faces once through windows glanced, cheek to stone
　　Was laid and so remained, as once the sigh
　　　　Of hushed moat-water yielded love's assent.

Naught's fled: we Questers live! – alone
　　Beyond the chaliced valley, over Wye
　　　　Where dreams in silent woods the Land of Gwent.

St Briavels Castle, 1942

BELS EREMBORS

Whenas the lengthening days betoken May
The Knights of France ride home from far away.
Raynauz is there, he, pacing in the lead
'Neath Eremborès window bends his way,
And yet he never deigns to lift his head.
    Ai! Raynauz, love!

At window, Erembors, in the clear day,
Sits, knees o'erspread with bright embroidery.
She sees the Knights of France from far away,
Sees Raynauz, he, pacing in the lead,
And calls aloud, the first words in her head:
    "Ai! Raynauz, love!

"Lov'd Raynauz, how oft hast known the day
"When 'neath my father's tower, bending your way,
"You griev'd, if Erembors lack'd word for thee."
– "Emperor's daughter, wrong'st thou me all way:
"Another lovest, hast forgotten me."
    Ai! Raynauz, love!

"Raynauz, my Lord, thy true Love's true faith hear:
"One hundred sainted maidenheads I'll swear
"And thirty of my Dames shall witness bear
"I love but thee, and no man aught is there.
"Take this my pledge: take these my kisses, dear."
    Ai! Raynauz, love!

The Count Raynauz has clomb the castle stair.
Wide at the shoulder, at the baldric spare,
The crisp beard well curled, yellow his hair.
In what land find so fair a bachelor?
She sees her love. She weeps to see him there.
    Ai! Raynauz, love!

The Count Raynauz is come into the tower
And set him on a couch besprent with flowers.
Fair next her Fair sitteth his Erembors.
Thus framed the twain, within Dan Cupid's bower,
Repeat the tales of love they told of yore.
    Ai! Raynauz, love!

Chanson de Toile, Anonymous,
12th century

'JE VOUS ENVOIE UN BOUQUET...'

To you I send these flowers that have not long
Of open petals woven left my hand,
I gathered them about the evensong –
Tomorrow would have strewn them o'er the land.

Then let this be to you a certain sign
Of how your beauties, now in perfect flower,
Shall in a little wither & decline
And fall, as petals do, within the hour.

Time! Time, my sweetheart, time is slipping by.
Ah! 'tis not time, but we alone who go
And underneath the stone extended lie.

Then since our loves, of which we now speak so,
When we are dead the world will quite forget,
Come, love me now, whiles thou art lovely yet.

Ronsard

LITANY OF THE HEART

Accept these tokens in exchange of hearts.
Mine heartsease flowereth fast in ink.
Bright blossoms burst from my penmarks.

Heart of blood be in me.
Heart of water whisper in me.
Heart of silver moon pity me.
Heart of yellow sun kindle me.
Heart of space fill me.
Heart of silences speak to me.
Heart of glass consider me.
Heart of green protect me.
Heart of pitch engulf me.
Heart of white blind me.
Heart of tall places humble me.
Heart of the abyss ennoble me.
Heart of Stone quiet me.
Heart of Rose enfold me.
Heart of Hearts beat in me.

Heart of spring leap in me.
Heart of summer stretch in me.
Heart of autumn yawn in me.
Heart of winter sleep in me.
Heart of hours cherish me.
Heart of days fashion me.
Heart of years emprison me.
Heart of earth soil me.
Heart of rains wash me.
Heart of fire burn me.
Heart of air caress me.
Heart of life impregnate me.
Heart of death impregnate me.
Heart of Stone quiet me.

Heart of Rose enfold me.
Heart of Hearts beat in me.

Heart of hills summon me.
Heart of roads lure me.
Heart of cities spurn me.
Heart of fields laugh in me.
Heart of tree grow in me.
Heart of corn dance in me.
Heart of gardens rest in me.
Heart of flowers blush for me.
Heart of bird sing in me.
Heart of nightfall blink at me.
Heart of darkness stroke me.
Heart of dawn stir in me.
Heart of light enshrine me.
Heart of Stone quiet me.
Heart of Rose enfold me.
Heart of Hearts beat in me.

Heart of child trust me.
Heart of man comfort me.
Heart of woman receive me.
Heart of Stone quiet me.
Heart of Rose enfold me.
Heart of Hearts beat in me.

FOR MUSIC

Lay between your smooth
                        thighs
his face and soothe
with fingers small,
dreams
        curled where that wound lies.
The running grass no sound gives,
each bough, blossom of this ground
keeps love's secrecy,
                        all
occluded from what seems
of love,
        the word, the splintering light,
        the empty glass, the bright
        attentive love-look
        the down-turned book,
know
in the grave shade only of your own midnight
        the dove
                love
                        sighs.

A RECIPE

Greengage, apricot & plum
bursting out of blossom come,
whose bold buds have melted glue
last year's sap had set anew.
Round the bole & on the twig
roving wasp & brown earwig
menace apple, pear & peach
hung beyond your slender reach.
Set the ladder up & pluck
where stripling wasp & earwig suck
white & yellow juices meeter
for a cooking pie & sweeter
in my mouth & on your tongue
or under cider barrel's bung.
For cheeks & cherries, eyes & lips
are like Dame Beeton's preserve tips,
they wrap in such confusion Time
as pastries when the taste of lime
un-corked or -bottled out of age
startles away the sour years' ravage.
... Foot on ladder, mount the rung
your startling flesh will burn
     as old when young.

THE EMPTY HOUSE

Melodiously
a hazel sky
weeps gloom.

Empty the house
gone all carouse,
the room

slyly mutters
whose gay shutters
new stained

with autumn weather
echo together.
We lay

on earthen floor,
unlatched the door,
our play

dumb to the world.
Slowly unfurled
the sky

earth, walls, roof, you
receded, "Who
in my

hands heaved?" he asked,
and you, bruised, tasked
the cry...

or, with older love
plucked at remove
the shaft

deftly unlocked
the gates, high cocked
him,
    and laughed.

APPEARANCE(S)

As the eye resolves
        distances
this pool resolves
        clouds
that appear
        to pass
& tree
        (hanging etc.)
that appears
        not to.

Mud / cloud
        tree / water
forever
        the image
bearing
        its own
impingement:

Nor can you
        wipe
whose shadow
        from your skin
nor brush
        whose face
from
        (irresolute

(where all hangs
        eyes

THE ELM-TREE WALK

Place of summer trysts,
tryst-marks cut
in the elm-tree's bole.

Tall elms
dark in the high branches
where autumn dusk settles in.

All day,
bewildering the air
a maze of leaves drifts

Down across the elm-tree walk,
sheaves of the coruscated year
shaken loose

Settling on the ground
& on your shoulders
& leaf-like hair

Where you (bewildered) stand
waiting, as once,
for one who does not come

Nor shall, though you outstay
autumn's leave-taking,
and hips, haws, red berries show
winter begun.

CODEX VERONENSIS

      Wine stains the verse –
the curse of time obliterates the arrogant line.

Then, in Verona, Campesani knows
the 'Roman hand':
"One woman could command
this song."
         He sang
and fourteen hundred years
later, it reappears –
         in the barrel's bung
(the hand that Campesani knows)
codex from wine-bung springing
as from the dung
         – the rose.

THE SHAKTA BRIDE

The shakta bride waits by the river at nightfall.
The shakta bride waits by the dark waters.
I shall go down to the dark waters.
I shall go down to the river at nightfall.
Smothered in the forests of my own heart
I can still watch and wait.
I will shake off my clothes.
Folding myself in the silence
I shall sit on my heels and wait.
She, she will come over the wide meadows,
     shaking the grasses,
Her arm curved to the pitcher on her head.
Kneeling together, we shall stretch out our hands.
We shall engage in the dark waters in silence.

PARMENIDES & THE LOOKING-GLASS

*The poet secretly imprints his own image
in his mistress' looking-glass.*

If old Parmenides was right
and all remains, though lost to sight,
those looks you keep for one alone
are not as chaste as they might own.

The treasured lashes, lids & hair
preserved as matrimonial fare
with constant opposites each day
commingle in adulterous play:

Each lovely item sprung from dust,
the lower lip that spells out lust,
the sockets, bone & moulded skin
rehearse a *pas de deux* with sin.

For what is it pervades the grace
diffusing from your curious face
but that within your looking-glass
a strange face waits for yours to pass.

Twin eyes to eyes, twin lips to lips,
one face into the other slips,
osmosis by ourselves unfelt
we two into each other melt.

You sit and with cosmetic art
set those soft eyes more wide apart,
with humour & eye-shadow blue
re-emphasise the 'essential you'.

Then rise, but as you walk downstairs
accept this secret in your ears –

those looks that from the glass you're lent
the dalliance, dearest, are
                    of love, not paint.

ON THE PIER

Honey of memory distilled
        from head scissored on broken water
where crests spill salt over topaz
        over green, over blue: alone on the pierhead
separate from the schizoid hordes,
        from the beach, the traffic & single
people ambling in kaleidoscopic patterns
        along the promenade, or who disappear
like sunblown shadows abruptly
        up the sexy sidestreets of the front,
we stand on the iron grille
        while the sea watches us from below.
You remove your absurd shoes,
        your dress is turquoise and
there are turquoise bobbles on the shoes,
        the sea also – all colours – is turquoise
while your eyes, green (topaz in cross-glint),
        watch the reflection of your speech
& actions in my chopped, happy
        gestures which you share,

and we, indeed, for that time share
    each other's selves in full view
of sky, of summer crowds & sea.

    So this poem, dear, this page
of statements beyond themselves
    read: of you, the plebeian pier
the broken sea... while time crumbles.
    And one more thought: your hair.
Of amber melting the cold wind.
    Is here a picture of what
a life of unfulfilled desire
    can make of such as you?
Or, as a grown-up's toy, life
    precious as ambergris, sweet as honey
forced by such hunger to become
    the image of your impulsive veins –
icon: holy food.

from Clear Lake Comes from Enjoyment

THE ORCHARD IS NOT CUT DOWN

The orchard is gone. A space con-
    ventionally like Passchendaele,
    linearly framed by black rail-
ings, rises to a wide field on
which, inert, the milk-brown cows sun
    themselves and where the busy mail-
    van and the bus brightly curtail,
on the road sudden as a gun,
the field – the vanished grove.

            No dream
    of priest or king can empower mind
    to seize the blossom on the wind;
only, in passing, I have seen

    swan leaning on confused swan
    fall inwards like a folding fan.

THE REFLOWERING

When this flame, this vital spark, this life that is us,
Suddenly goes out

When the Spirit of our flesh
Disappears

When *You* cease from our knowing
Or from our way of knowing

Consider the fire on the bough.

When blood, water, the body's moisture
Evaporates

When the tissues of flesh
Shrivel

And the slender sun-golden limbs,
Foot, hand, face,
                    disintegrate

Consider the fire on the bough,
Consider the daffodil flame,
Consider the flower-knots that pattern the orchard grasses
Before the blossom has yet come.

When the flame is quenched
And your fingers no longer move over the familiar objects,
When your imprint is invisible in the armchair,
And the outline of your body
Standing so finely in the garden
Is at once real and illusory,
When your spirit disappears
And *You* cease from our knowing,

We can use but the worn phrases of sorrow
And we say, "When the flame is quenched..."
Or, "When the echoes have settled..."
"When the last ripple is stilled...".
It is the natural language of sorrow,
These pictures of space & time.
                              – And of them?
... A way of experiencing eternity.

When the body dies
The subsistent forces of the body,
The forces of tension within the atom,
Reform in the stalk, leaf, petal.

Your Spirit reappears.
It is the Spirit of a Japanese cherry.

                              Or a snail.

And we say a cadence has closed.
But this is not so.
There can be no addition to Heaven.

Remember the bright buds.
Consider the fire on the bough.

NEST OF CUNNUS

In sylvan Land-
    seer portrait scape
    a maiden stands
whom no escape
    from formal frame
    of classic rape
can spare for shame.
    Morality
    of guilt or blame
must stem from free
    alternatives.
    This swing, that tree
those virgin lives
    are states at which
    their end connives.
The lovers' itch
    can hardly know
    what little bitch
or saintly sow
    their mutual bliss
    will turn into.
First, come, that kiss!
    then 'neath this hedge
    where bullocks piss
yield up that wedge
    of softest flesh
    and he will dredge
through the silk mesh
    under the thatch
    where your warm, lush
fields closely lie.

Burst the picture
      with your flanks; call
      moral stricture
over the wall;
      rope in the Choice
      that God let fall:
Let outside in
      and it will come
      purged free of sin –
cleanly welcome.

So he'll divide
      your thatch and catch
      on either side
the startled fish
      revealing wide
      his open wish,
maculate bride.

On the fresh grass
      accept the sun,
      all flesh is glass
in his benison –
      all colours pass
      where his beams run.
Pull up your gown,
      the lightest one
      of these light down
hairs throbs in him,
      as, hard in you,
      now bright, now dim,
one stiffly lies.

      This solar force
      knows no remorse
and brief tranquillity.

CONKER AVENUE

I must start with the red road of the avenue,
And the chestnut trees on either side.
The stars turn on their axes
And the leaves fall   and now the tops of tall trees
Like broomsticks sorrowfully brush the sky.
                                        And I?
In the morning and at the evening
Walk regularly along the red road of the avenue
With the chestnut trees on either side
And the two lines of black fencework beyond.
Upon the one hand there is an orchard
And on the other landskip and scape dip
Wrinkle and roll fold and unfold
To far away tree-crested hills of chalk.
In the orchard, where hangs a solitary apple
Glued to a twig (the crimson heart of the wood)
Symmetrical bunches and balls of mud-coloured twigs
Riddled with the grey skylight of a winter's afternoon
Top the twisted trunks of the apple trees.

Between the landscape and the orchard
With the chestnut trees on either side
The avenue runs from the school – of green cupolas
And crenellated turrets stamped on a dirty sky –
To a house... a little house.
Here are the great gates with the heraldic birds,
Claw foot, carved beak and feathered stone,
Poised above a tracery of wrought ironwork,
Phoenix or Griffin posing the question,
A-level with the brushwork of the trees
Posed, poised... ?resolving the answer
At the red road's hesitant pause.

Thus through the morning and the evening of the four
     seasons
As the stars turn and the leaves fall
I walk along the red road of the avenue
And these are the images through which I move.

And now I have come to my chief difficulty,
The difficulty of writing at all.
It is of these images, these beads – coloured balls –
I would make my radiant node or cluster,
But the tenuous thread frays
And the bright bead-balls splay, fall, out into darkness
Silently.

          (The chestnut trees sprout candles in the spring.
In spring weather the white candles of the chestnuts
Light me my way...)

Is it alone in the starless reaches of the soul that things
     cohere?

I will fix in a timeless pattern
Bare dry irreducible facts:
Let the mute birds (enigmatic guardians)
Hang by the gates in motionless flight
Let the crimson fruit be a-glow in a winter's day
Let the cupolas be – the turrets – the taller trees
Let tall trees slide sadly under a low sky
Let others be moved as I am moved by these things.

I walk by the red road.
The chestnut trees glide past me one by one.
The red soil moves beneath my feet.
I strive with intuitive vision
To pierce haphazard juxtaposition.
And rumours of the heart assail me.

CLEAR LAKE COMES FROM ENJOYMENT

Clear lake comes from enjoyment.
The ripe fig bursts.

In the garden
heat clothes all: the pinks & lupins in the border,
the drooping lime whose sticky leaves dangle above your
    hair.
You sit on the old bench unobserved. Apart
from the roll of flesh pushing
comfortably out around the waist
(for you are no longer young, nor
do you deeply care about such things),
your white blouse & striped summer skirt
hang loosely over your open arms & legs.
The shin-bones shine, and the light hair
glistens with small sweat. Ankles & wrists
quite still, the bones moulding the drawn skin.

What imbroglio is here?
How say, poor ape, you know another from yourself?
Is strangeness all the lure, and love an Indian trick
where bride & bridegroom jump into each other?
Speak, over the lawn, my love,
and say, where is my love?

My love, I am the clothes you wear,
the lime-leaf brushing your dark hair,
across your bone, the fine skin,
the crimson fig consumed within,
the bather in the hidden pool,
the dreamer winding the enchanted spool.

PRIAPUS

I dedicate, I consecrate this grove to thee,
Priapus, whose home & woodlands are at Lampsacus;
there, among the coastal cities of the Hellespont,
they chiefly worship thee:
                    their shores are rich in oysters!

                           attributed to Catullus

LE JARDIN DE LA POÉSIE

I THE MAKING

What the tongue cannot tell
What the eye cannot see
What the ear cannot hear
What the flesh cannot feel
The mind cannot know.

"Poetry is the subject of the poem."
Naturally.

      For the struggle
To communicate the incommunicable
To see the invisible
To hear the inaudible
To feel the intangible
To think with the heart
Is the stuff of poetry.

And so it is natural that poetry
Should be the subject of every poem –
And that the poem should never be written.

The slick telephonist controls
    Ecstatic wires of flesh & blood,
Who underneath her camisoles
    Permits the logic of the Flood.

Manipulatrix behind the scenes!
    Would tyrannise our daily life;
Herself conditioned by her genes,
    The essence of her husband's wife.

The barren logic which she wields
    Can premise only what she knows.
Experience of ghostly fields
    Where the fadeless amaranth blows

Cannot be for her as us:
    We have known aesthetic stasis –
She has 'known' Democritus,
    And forgotten what her place is:

A lady of undoubted parts,
Barely a handmaid of the arts.

III GARDEN

So, see, the morning sunlight slides over the fir-tree tops
And spreads itself in the far corner of the garden.
I do not walk much in the garden in the morning,
But lying in bed see the great stone birds,
With their attendant birds twinkling about them;
And at eight o'clock I can hear Mr Pike.
He wheels his bicycle beneath our bedroom window.
He is slashing the laurels and letting in the wide field.
The field grasses are a yellowy green: it is dry summer;
All day long they shiver and change colour,
Like velvet under a stroking hand.
They enfold two sides of the garden,
And the fir trees shut off the quiet road.
Nothing is there of which a man could in any way be proud:
No stonework, no statuary nor playful fountain,
But a stone pathway dividing a rectangular plot of earth
Where weeds, nettles, vegetables & flowers flourish
　　　indifferently.

Mr Pike has an acquaintance with moles & field-mice
And the curious secretive animals which are alive in our
　　　garden.
He can gauge the power of the sun underground.
He understands the white root wriggling in the darkness.
He is grey-headed, short & square,
And he lays his hands flat on his stained shirt
As he says: "Thet apple woan't bear noa fruit
This year, nor anywen."
　　　　　　　　　　I observe that there are no apples,
And that the three trees are standing around awkwardly
　　　here & there,
Waiting for Mr Pike to cut them down.
But we shall not allow Mr Pike to cut them down,
For without them the garden might suddenly look like itself:

A corner of the wide field which somebody has dug up.
In spring the apple trees have apple blossom red & white,
And delicate petals detach themselves from among cool
    leaves,
Loosen themselves from between still boughs,
Only the hesitant air, guiding the fall of them,
Checks their virginal flight.

The sun rolls towards the meridian.
The vegetable leaf broadens & glows.
The light flows with the sap.

Under moving veils of the summer wind
You cannot see but you may feel
The slow thrust & pressure of vegetable life,
Dance of the stem, twig, blossom & leaf,
Immobile in the figures of their dance.

The soil is turned & the hedge trimmed.
A bunch of large-petalled peonies has been handed in at
    the back door
And, as afternoon sinks into evening, Mr Pike collects his
    tools
And wheels his bicycle around the side of the house.
I walk out into the garden and stand on the stone pathway.
The field-grasses are now blue; the fir trees black.
Stealthily the heavy shadows of all still things
Begin to snuff the daylight out of the warm air.

Sometimes at this hour I wonder
Who among my friends would wish to share
These quiet influences with me. Few, I fear,
For Jefferson designed Palladian palaces;
Santayana lacked simplicity of heart,
And was a trifle too detached;
Chaucer, I doubt; Pope, not; the shining Byron, not;
And Yeats, we are told, 'dreamed of nobility'.

But Thoreau would have been most happy here;
And those contemplative, quiet men,
John Clare, Parson Barnes, Thomas Hardy,
And Hueffer too, – strange in their company.

When I have conversations in my garden in the evening,
It is with these few.
They stand around under the faint boughs of the apple trees,
Or on the stone pathway beside me.

It grows cool.
           Pale stars appear in the sky.
The encroaching field ebbs mysteriously away.
The fat marrow glimmers in the darkness.

CLIO: The Muse of History – rational knowledge – the Mind
CALLIOPE: The Epic Muse – traditional or instinctive
    knowledge – the Heart
TERPSICHORE: The Muse of the Dance – intuitive or
    direct knowledge – the Soul

SELF
Ladies,
I enquire wherein your influences reign,
    What functions you envisage with yourselves,
    How the mind, heart & soul can best retain
Those functions, in the place where the mind shelves
    To the heart, heart to soul, where mind, heart, soul
    Can scarce discern each other from themselves.

CLIO
My sphere is human reason.

CALLIOPE
                    I control
The modes of prejudice & instinct.

TERPSICHORE
                    I
    The act of intuition, when the goal
And the desire are one.

SELF
                Do you then lie
Within the Psyche, or does she in you?
And, whoso shines in whom, can we descry,
As by intensity of starlight, who
    Serves Truth, serves Goodness, and who bright Beauty?

CLIO

I shall answer. Know that myself & these two
Nymphs are facets of the Psyche: our duty
    To deflect our skills on to her dark sphere;
    For the Psyche's principal attribute
Is a recipience, felt or no; her
    Being, a fullness of our informing powers.
Blessed doubtfully with soul man can aver,
By cultivating & selecting our
    Intelligence, his ethos is his fate.
The proportions of created things reflower
In cerebration, which is disparate
    From love & intuition in that they
    Are one & two & hard to correlate.

CALLIOPE

Reason, providing instinct with its mainstay,
    Is then transcended by its own effect.

CLIO

Which is but rational habit come to stay –

CALLIOPE

Habit, or predilection, where respect
    Of love & of the modes of the affections
    Lurks innately.

TERPSICHORE

                    Nor has instinct that direct
Knowledge born of will on instinct: intuition,
    In which the Psyche – soul & heart & mind –
    Is in the object of her contemplation,
It in her, hypostatically entwined.
    Trajectories of lover & beloved
    Which heart alone erratically inclined,
Which the brain first heartlessly misled
    Skewing each one awry from other's kind,

Are in the soul unalterably wed.
Beneath the operations of the will,
  Liver & heart resign themselves to soul
  Whose conditions of direct knowledge fill
And irreparably affect the whole
  Psyche.

SELF
  Then, since in you I must fulfill
  My work & self, and knowledge is control
Of reason, let Terpsichore instill
  Herself within myself, sending her glance
  Through me as I pursue to their conclusion
Images of the interweaving dance,
Transfixed in her, its own resemblance.

V IMAGE

In fading light
    with tangled rays
    twin pairs of eyes
refract delight.

We lean & stare.
    The kiss is in
    the lover's skin,
refract despair

o baffled eye.
    I lean & stare
    through her to where
is naught but I
unendingly.

        * * *

Rose-red has shed
    her colours, gone,
    gone stick & stone
in darkness crumbled.

There is the moment of arrest
And the act of arresting
The moment of arrest,
– *En noche oscura.*

Lover & beloved in their crystal spheres
Assume their formal radiance and remain.

Truly is our life a dying fall,
As water, glancing, falls like watered silk,
As the leaf falls,
And the grass grows where the leaf has fallen.

And they would say:
                "The force that keeps the stars &
        moves the Heavens
Moves that man."
                And: "There goes one who has walked
        in Hell," they said.

And he had watched her walking through the streets.

O words O vows O gifts O tears O sacrifice.

DINING-OUT

In country snow last night we joined the horde
    Of diners-out;
                ('Bali' upon the wall.)
    "You've come! How good you are! You know us
      all ..."
Motionless beneath the menacing sword
We wait the revelation of the word.
      The talk is small, the accent trivial:
      "Beryl, I hear, has done one on Nepal."
The golden firelight lights the shrunken board.

Bawd! Your chemistry is intellectual:
      What man is there of English social life
      Could satisfy Ashoka's hundredth wife?
What shakta bride of 'obscene' ritual?
      What shaven loins does that coarse Harris hide?
      Who wears the grave sarong – that does not 'ride'?

54

HOMAGE TO EZRA POUND

Since 2,800 years, Homer is dead;
His mouth more often filled with verses than with bread.
A-squat on the sun-hot stone, in the glare,
Blind to the lyrical sun,
And a blind man's fingers light on the sensitive lute.
Still, still the polysyllabled sea-rush rolls to our shores;
The singing voice is mute.

Lo! Ferlies befalleth where is love-gladness,
'Neath moon-sleight in orchard when pierceth love's
    madness.
Silken the song, spun of air, in the dew,
Tense with the immanent muse,
And coins & castles, heaulmes & politics their song.
Where now are the stones? Where is the bright hair of
    those women?
Gone, all, the long-gone dead among.

Dante Alighieri! Impelled by Love & led
By Wizardry, his death-mask hangs above my bed.
Pre-Raphaelite the work, the laurel leaves
Parnassian, smutched with gilt.
Pale eyes burned in the ivory stillness of that face;
Clothed in a white geometric vision, he stalked
Unsoiled through the market-place.

Dan Chaucer next, our 'fount of English undefiled',
And would he, from his customs house, have smiled
At such a laurel, so bestowed?
Here is there no aroma
Of Dutch cloth, or coarse-grained bags of spice,
But an air as of conversations with Boccace,
And memory of Provence.

Ravens by starshine, by sunlight, in wind, in rain,
Have pecked poor Francis Villon skin & bone again.
Shrivelled the restless tongue, the nicked lip;
Empty the mock-lit eye.
Sunlight spills pattern of rose on cathedral floor;
Seine breaks under bridges; dark firelight & laughter
Leap from the tavern door.

The names fall now as in the roll-call of Dead Lords:
Douglas, Golding, Pope, each of glittering word-hoards.
Savage Landor, that ancient Roman,
Wrote for seventy years in stone.
The recent laureate, Browning happily shares
With Hardy, who endowed puppets with nobility,
And Yeats, that pursuer of arcane hares.

And old Ez, folding his blankets in Pisan meadows,
Unlocked his word-hoard, as of this troop of shadows.
You who have walked, by Cahors, by Chaluz,
Made Odyssean landfall,
Your voice is as old as the first dead in my song,
And would you might perceive herein, such strength in
    gentilesse,
Such subtlety, as tips your tongue.

CODA TO SAPPHO

Bend, bend to the bars, whence that white glow flusheth
    your face,
Source of a heat more subtle, more destructive, and less harm-
    ful than true fire which bronze consumes.

For fire, that ravisher, knows no destructive spell, no charm
So potent as the firelit trance your love-gaze casts
    In quivering interspace.

Wind, revealer of thighs, importunate wind! Stamp so your
    shape
On his encircling stream, that thence, for aftertime, such
    trace
    Of thee the blackest wind may warm.

Water, speller of destinies, moved by the moon. Is foam- lace
Spread upon flesh-coral, whipped white about red? The
    moist palm,
    The bronzed foot is engendered.

* * *

Former kings & cities lost in the valley of your arm.
Sloth is hurtful to me. Sloth indeed is my bane, – and thine,
    O my Catullus!

THE MIRROR

In her discreet room
A mirror hangs by the door,
And on the days when I am received
I regard her

Pause for a moment – incline
(With subtle accentuation of hip)
To the door-handle,
Absently holding herself
In the brief glass.

And I have wondered
If she remarks
What you & I (my friend)
Have so often remarked to each other.
Does she remark these things?

My God!
Doesn't anyone know
What this beautiful woman is thinking
As she goes through the door?

ADONIA

"Those men who immediately think a woman
is meant only for *that*,
                              who transfix you
like a butterfly with their masculine minds..
How boring!"
                    The eyebrows curved,
                              brown eyes sweeping
the cheek-line,
                    the small hand pressed
between the breasts, *agitato*.
And he said:
                    "No one could transfix you,
even as the most beautiful butterfly."
And he looked at the fair hair bowed above the brandy-whip
– "But not 'boring'," he thought. "Never 'boring'.
                              Certainly not *that*!"

THE FIRST HYMN

Hestia will tend my fire
And Hermes the ways about my house.

Rose & myrtle & poppy fall toward the sea.
The small waves come & go on the sand.

I have watched the white-breasted swan parting the waters.
I have seen the swallow disentangling in flight its shadow.

Rose-blown, sea-born of Cerigo,
Apple queen,
                myrtle-wreathed,
Thou, heavy with dreams at the corn season.

Hestia tends my fire
And Hermes the ways about my house.
Your statue stands
                to the seaward
Where rose & myrtle & poppy fall toward the sea,
Where the small waves smile in your countenance,
Where the small waves dance upon the sand.

The Ingathering of Love

THE INGATHERING OF LOVE

What can I hope for from this love of mine:
to live another's life
                be you
walk in your raincoat in wet country lanes
stretch in your chair
or feel the grape squirt against your teeth?

Vignettes of firelit or of summer evenings,
of autumn
           when the shiftless skies move out of tune
when the trees ache
and a damp air endistances the nearby fields:
What can I hope for from this love of mine?

All day the willow weeps by the summerhouse.
Bits of grass, the detritus of summer, lie on the floor;
the birds are muted
              appeased by nest-building & egg laying:
a plane fades like mild thunder and
the sun, an atmosphere, pervades the grey sky.

Walk on precarious heels across the sodden lawn,
old clothes, hair anyhow,
– the sun will not come out. No:
but traces of that lightning struck
from your eyes, a day now years ago
flicker from where you walk.

So bird rose tree lawn
rearrange themselves
             the ambience changes

all is framed for you,
and you, the picture, blank to other eyes.

This melancholy autumn light
the shielding trees
                lime oak fir
the wild herbaceous border
                        – all indifferent
only you and I electrify the scene.
Then the worm gnaws with a purpose.
The petal flutters knowingly to its end.

The way you hold your cigarette
                                or cross your legs
the heavy smell of too much powder after sleep
the way you drink your drink
                        these ways we start
to play with sex.
                "Sit with me here in this deck-chair."
The nostalgic sun remembers younger flesh
with gentler lines.
                Ah, these are the chains
the taffeta petticoats & gleaming hair
the sex-toys that we start with when we say
"What fun to scratch her crisp bun
of hair, slide down that old furrow…"
The toys of love become Love's armoury
when the tickling's over.

Hours have passed, and you
do not come round the corner of the house.
A few birds have woken up, crying shrilly;
as darkness slips between the branches
the roses in the rose-bed glow
                        white pink yellow –

gathering the colours they have displayed by day
back to the night.

When all is so evidently separate
there must be some very good reason
for this feeling we all have
that life is somehow, mysteriously, one.

"Let me in," the angel cries at the door.
"Let me in," moans the ghost to the virgin.
Unfurl the petal. Let the fountain play whitely.
Is it here, that ashen pillar?

And God said to God, "Let Me love You."
(He had to double back on Himself for that.)
"Let me in," tree cries to tree, bird to sky.
"Come over here and I will show you something,"
the small boy whispers to his little sister.
"Let me in."
                    And the sage is indubitable:
The presence does indeed inhabit the dark cave.

In a word
            (self-delivered & time-grieved)
it is all the love we have
to take a header into the pool
to embrace yourself in yourself

where the fountain shoots

and the darkness can only be unrelieved.

The birds are all flying one way. Often
I have seen them gathering for migration or
sitting & talking about it
                    — but never actually flying away.
They are all flying over the trees, purposefully...
and a cloudlike haze slides off in the same direction.

Despite the persistent dew soaking my bedroom slippers
and the trees limp from too much summer
like women, love over
putting their soiled clothes off
thankful to be alone with their own nakedness...
despite all signs of a final departure
autumn has caught us unawares.

— And our love?...
Will it pass in some cloud of euthanasia?
Or like the birds?
Or will you, undressing one day
resignedly placing slip bra stockings over the chair
turn
        stripped of my desire
sheathed
            as in childhood again
in your own nakedness?

Our laughter that evening fell like leaves in autumn.
Afterwards, we went out to the car
and stars were shining in the wet sky.

What 'prognosis of divinity'
what 'synchronicity of occasions'
could have called you here
to the great gates where the avenue inconclusively ends,

where the chestnut trees lit from our warm windows
seem weighted with 'lieder' airs.

We stand for a moment by the car door.
(My arm is about a waist.)
And you leave
                in a perfect diminuendo.

A wind stirs coldly –
Here is not *here*
: always there,

as those stars, now, are not here,
but light,
        aeons of years ago.

Nearly always it happens unawares.

There are winter winds in the dark
                                – the rain spitting outside
and the little hall littered with wellington boots
                                        umbrellas
                                        children's toys
you stoop, tidying something away in a corner
we have left the fire and the light
the music playing
                the books open on the armchairs
you stoop to put something away in a corner
as defenceless as the two tendons stretched at the back of
    your legs
your hair (a bit greasy)
                        falling over your face
and you chuck your head up

and our eyes
        customarily veiled against the unforeseen
        become suddenly the source
        of what we have foreseen
        & then
            not begun to see.

Later, we'll meet with veiled eyes
seated at supper
        or in the garden
surrounded by objects I have known & you have touched.

        Momentarily
        love lies bared in a look.
        Still, where you are
        lightning cloaks the scene.

Writing poetry is like having the curse:
it can take you anywhere.
The living tissue secretes
        and comes away
and is thrown in the waste bin.
Only when the conjunction is favourable
can the egg take life,
        will the dark globule swell,
and the full poem erupt in us.

This moment by the door
how warm, tender and mysterious
it will seem
        twenty years on!
They will be fingering some yellowed snap,

my collar will look awkward
your hair, funny.

The light now fails
and a pigeon flies low over that hedge.
It has been a day of opaque sunlight,
the mist clearing at about ten.
The deck chairs were left out all night
and when we came to them in the morning
we found twenty or thirty leaves
crisp, pale brown, turned inwards
heaped in the striped seats.

The sky is expressionless.
On the lawn, the paraphernalia of amusement
are discarded,
diaphanous oyster of silk
fades as I watch.

The same pigeon flies back (low) to its nest
and a grey gauze settles over the landscape...

The evening wind still pushes onwards.

This is the way men will remember me,
not in the moments on the bed,
(or on the floor)
not, certainly, on the telephone
(the assured or pitiful manipulation)
not in the vinousness of relaxed suppers,
or the sickening fragmentation before dawn,
not even in my daughter's face,
the eyelid which earth & sky & the fierce years
will crush.

Does the dove in the oak recall Dodona,
or the cherry tree the mountain of Zen?
On the still lawn we shall be seen,
where the sunlight is still as the leaning apple trees,
where the spring wells
and its glittering accidents hold the essential air,
where the concealed birds
weaving a hedge of song
enclose this place and this hour.

Through trees
          where we have thinned the lower branches
the two fields slope towards each other.
In November rain
                    we'll walk in the valley dip
the air thick around us.
                    No time
before we knew each other, or
for one of us, again, alone.
"Only today is ours."
Your rose-thorns bruise my lips,
how can I know them minus tongue and teeth?
What trace
          (malign or otherwise)
can busy hands, legs, our bodies
secret as the lowering air
leave?

Wet, in November rain,
          we skewered that terror squarely on our tongues.
Love like the air around us,
the absurdity of disbelief shining
in the endless movement to-and-fro
                    of eyes
cast between your image and my gaze.

Hold me & let go.
            Feel in your raincoat pockets,
your profile cut against the stream in the field's dip.
Our mirror lines diverge,
                  the broken tension
quivers on the air,
                  a trace remaining
neither malign nor otherwise,
                  a context, merely – something natural
to the next couple walking in the same field.

You are sitting by the firelight in concealed splendour
            swiftly and intricately sewing
                  your mind – elsewhere
or on a path where honeysuckle grows
            aimless in a blaze of sun
            your hair a part of the sunlight
                  standing

or after a journey
                  in the close lull
                  lighting a cigarette
                  slipping from one pair of shoes into another
before you reach for the car door
and we both turn and again –
                  reject life

or it may be that I am standing by the fire, talking
and you walk over to the fireplace
handing me a drink
                  offering me a cigarette
and I am at once involved in your legs, arms, throat;
            your body an almond
                  glows through the gauze of cotton or shantung,
and you, knowing what you have done,

take with candour my face among your warm snows,
so that I close my eyes
so that the snowstorm whirls in my head.

Smoke on the Moscow sky
trails from factory chimneys.
The walls of the Potala Palace slope
upwards & inwards – no chimneys.
The indifferent green of our asbestos garage
carries, while the sun gleams,
a restless web of different green.
Remote walls, endlessly grey skies,
and this sunlit movement
where the foliage sprawls.

When the darker air emerges
with a disarming stealth
from the canopy of the great trees,
the grass, the wheelbarrow & the play-pit
are infused with a closeness unsuspected in the day.

And men in overalls
walking pavements in the Urals
glimpse the New World skyline,
cold pillars, saline monuments.

When day breaks, a mist of pale leaves
obscures that medium-sized beech tree,
and Shiva with a hundred arms
writhes in the cloud.

It was in one of those old stone houses in Monmouthshire
that we first met.
                    The flagged kitchen
filled by a battered refectory table,
                              a whole family
sprawled there, gossiping...
                         and you walked in from a side door
– in a swathe of sunlight.

                    Was it farm eggs?
or something about cutting a hedge?
or one of those dances we all went to?
                         I recall
the impatient sun
                    through the low windows
describing your neck and chin;
                    I recall
how you walked
              & stood
free with your legs
                    as girls who have no thought of getting married
walk and stand,
                    gauchely, a little astride,
a light cotton skirt loose on your hips.
It is used by our children, now, for dressing up.
Laughing immoderately
                    they stumble about in its neglected folds;
pausing fractionally, they hesitate,
                              when the cloth suddenly tears.

That laughter is caught like tears in the groin
as the swirling Usk catches Caerleon
as we first caught hold of each other
                              thoughtlessly
with our tongues' and fingers' ends.

We could have lived no other life but this.

The centre drives.
                    The reef forms.
Your acts & mine.
                    A network of peripheries.
Never still.
            The coral blossoms.
The petals,
        in lovers' shoes,
in shopping baskets
                up the Woodstock & the Banbury road.
A world refracted in spring wind & rain.
Wet pavements
                lips & eyes
dissolving
        as the petals fall.
The weight of ocean,
                    almond & cherry
falling
        in the face of dreams.

We could have lived no other life but this.

In a student hostel off the Banbury road...
we came down afterwards to the party,
danced and talked with them all there.
In my eyes, still, the length of your body
and the dark triangle of hair. What student,
practised or not in love, sits on that hard
chair, lies on that bed?

The Dalai Lama is quite right:
knowledge is the act of being
when ignorance is the only sin.

The wind with bitter ardour
takes the blossom from the bough.

The small bird depositing its droppings on the garden
    bench
shifts its four claws
while the flanks above the match-stick legs pulsate in
    synchrony.
The pale green pheasant's egg – idle in the empty dyke.
The white washing flapping on the line.

And as skies parade overhead
the rainy garden momentarily fills with sunlight.

Alternatively:
        'the interstices of our flesh
are as much a part of our flesh
as our flesh?'
        Or, 'the rose
of menstrual blood in which the world is soaked.'

But no. Is there a doubt
the Dalai Lama knows the Dalai Lama
(knows) exactly what we are about.

Our bedroom darkens into light
                        the trees outside
their sap subsided
            adopt black attitudes,
a remote light
        looks in at the windows.

At this time,
        the flesh courses with fragmented images.
We enfold each other,
                seed stirs in the man.
The woman's stomach grows warm.
                        The fuse lit,
in the flare,
        God blinks at the bed.

And another dawn shall find you,
                        dry,
like the fruit you are,
                a carcass curled in this same bed,
your marred skin & eyes
glazed pools unstirred by otherness,
cloudy as these windows
where a brown haze now lies
in broad belts across the sky.
No light struck.
                No love.
Ash left with no fire.

And sunset & sunrise curtain the winter sky.
Here is love. And here is between hot bedclothes.
Here after all is where past & future lie.

The rolling heavens & the fire of time
consume this barrel body. Here,
the pitiably silent organs creep
blindly to decrepitude. The red water &
the blue gristle pale hourly,
                        – and somewhere/sometime
a fixed and ineluctable hour
an implacable and unavoidable wall
(on the other side of the bed

on the further side of the ward) – wait.
Strangers (indeed kind) must finally attend
this tiresome skinful, while self (as ever)
attends only the most idiot objects,
and the significance of the lifelong monologue
palls as life wanes.

              One observes, then, affectionate sunlight
melt unreal sugar on afternoon cakes,
– *They whipped hers out just in time!*
Hey Presto! (What dates one like slang?)
one is aware of the smell of linoleum
(sticky) whose surface sends back the black bed-legs
(on castors),
         one watches a helicopter hovering in a nearby field;
or the young man across the street removes the
silencer on his motor bike...
. . . .
                 Nothing,
nothing can shatter that silence.

There is the expectancy –
there is the revelation – of the bud;
or to turn with a gesture of wearied tenderness
to a worn head, the hair greying.
In the nursery the children are asleep and
the consciousness of their sleeping fills
the house. The skies turn. Time burns.

Yes. God will humble
              their silk skin
withdraw its flush
('the fever of life is over')

*   *   *   *   *

and leave that scrawny yellow.

Fourteen from Sappho

AGALLIDE

Equal to a god he seems who
sits listening to your sweet voice
& the sound of your Cyprian
          laughter that makes
my heart fail in my breast: I
have but to see you a little
and words die, an invisible
          flame laps at me
under my skin, I am tongue-tied,
my eyes see nothing & thunder
sounds in my ears, I sweat, shivering,
          pale as pale grass,
like a dead woman; Agallide,
it is this we must bear,
for so...

THE NIGHTINGALE

The lovers' nightingale that is
the clamorous angel of the spring

ORCHARD

Cool water among apple boughs...
sleep falling from quicksilver leaves

LOVE

The wind threshes the mountain oaks.
Eros is frenzied in the soul of Sappho.

Irresistible & bitter
the mastery that sweetly melts my limbs.

THE BRIDEGROOM

What can
Sappho
say you
are (my
husband
dearest)

– but the
rod of
supple
love-wood

stiffly
pliant?

THE LOOM

Talk to me,
Mother,
he comes
between
the loom
& me
... and
guileful
Venus
pricks me
with
        desire.

THE APPLE

The fruit-gatherers
    have forgotten
the reddest apple
    on the tree-top,
& the sweetest.
    Forgotten?
No, not forgotten,
    left...
too high to pick –

LONELINESS

Midnight,
    and the small hours
creep on,
    the Pleiads
& the Moon
    have set,
I lie alone.

FRIENDSHIP

Lay, sweet,
your head
against
the heart
of one
you love...

HER GIFTS

More music
        than the harp,
she yields,
        more gold
than gold...

OBLIVION

Sans record
     sans regret
you'll lie,
     who have no memory
of Pierian Roses:
     unknown
among the unknown dead
     your ghost
must go
     in the House of Dis.

THE MOON

The stars
     that circle
her bright face
       cloak theirs
when the night-queen
         sheds
her silver..
     light..
at the full

GIRLHOOD

Like
    the wild-
flower
      where
the shepherd's
         foot
treads
    and leaves
its petalled
      print

CHILDREN'S SONG

Childhood, childhood where have you gone?
Will you come back to us?
Will you come back?
Ever come back?

Never come back again.
Never come back.
Never.

Love Poems of the VIth Dalai Lama

NOTE

Only two Tibetan poets are at all well known outside their
own country: the eremite, Milarepa (1030–1115), and
Ts'angs-dbyangs-rgya-mts'o, who was the VIth Dalai Lama
(1683–1706). They are also the most widely read and best
loved in Tibet itself. Milarepa spent much of his life seated
in a state of semi-nudity among the snows of Everest, in
which situation he composed a large quantity of devotional
works. Ts'angs-dbyangs-rgya-mts'o came of ancient and
distinguished lineage. His family was a member of the Red
Cap sect. Unfortunately, his incumbency of the Lion Throne
proved less than edifying, though it had the merit, in the
circumstances, of being brief. Shortly after his solemn
consecration at the age of thirteen, the young pontiff began to
display a compulsive attraction for the pleasures of downtown Lhasa. By 1701, his aversion to the conventual dis-
ciplines of the Potala Palace had become a matter of scandal
and seemed likely to provoke political unrest. In order
to avert this, the Chinese Emperor, Kang-si, forced the
abdication of his spiritual, though not his temporal, pow-
ers. It may be thought that the renunciation was no great
loss to him. Five years later, in 1706, Kang-si had him
assassinated. However, the very qualities which marred and
finally destroyed his pontificate had the effect of endearing
him, in legend, to his people. The sixty-two poems, mostly in
four-line stanzas, called in English *The Love Songs of the VIth
Dalai Lama,* are known and loved all over Tibet. Priests
being priests (lamas, lamas) have endowed them with
spiritual significance, so that pious Tibetans can, if they
choose, read them a little as we read *The Song of Solomon,*
or the poems of St John of the Cross. Ts'angs-dbyangs-rgya-
mts'o did write orthodox religious works, but Tibetan
popular tradition does not hold that *The Love Songs* is among
them. The English poems which follow are not translations.
They are not paraphrases, interpretations, or even imitations.

91

They are simply 'poems suggested by'. The Tibetan text has been taken solely as a point of departure. The relation between the two can be seen by comparing one of the transcripts made for the author by a friend of his who is a Tibetan scholar, with the 'related' English poem (no. 26). The transcript runs: 'mind thither at lost having/night sleep order break/day-time in not receive/mind tire ... is it?/' Again, ferry-boats in Tibet often have carved on their prow a horse's head in reverse, so that the animal appears to be looking backwards; in the English poem (no. 20), the horse has come alive. And so on.

1

      This country girl
with skin like country cream
      looks with frankness
at me from the bed-furs.
      Her eyes watch me
put my rings on one side.
      They watch me
unlace my purse-belt.

2

White crane
   I need
      your wings
not
   for a long
      journey
over far
   mountains
      but only
a trip
   to Li-tang
      my home
(the rift
   of memory
      that
the trackers
   sought).

Return then
to Lhasa
in one week.

3

We have met in the valley of the South Forest
no eyes but yours & mine & bird eyes
among the branches. Talkative parrot
do not broadcast our happiness
from the cross-roads. Keep in your crop
the minutiae of our encounter,
the detail of gesture you have witnessed.

4

The moon emerges
from behind the East Mountains
and takes shape in my mind
like the memory of her mother's face
on the face of this girl.

5

A pattern of birds,
          crossed twigs,
& the last milestone
          have brought love
like luck
          to these two
met
          in this hedge-tavern,
where an old woman
          ladles out wine to them.

She will go on
        serving wine
on the periphery
        of their lives
at parting,
        at welcoming,
at childbirth.

6

This willow stands
        in your bailiwick
where none mutilates
        its yellow bark
or snaps off
        the grey green
leaves
        for luck
without risking
        a fine
from you,
        or at the least
a beating.
        Guard also
my girl's love-flag
        which flutters
in the sunny branches
        & the notes
& small tokens
        she shyly
mails me,
        here
where the trunk
        widens.

7

To be true to you
        is to be false
to who I am.
      To be true
to the self found in me
      is to be false
to an anxious woman.

8

Why does this pretty boy from Kong-po
buzz like a trapped bee?
He has been my bed-mate for three days,
and now he thinks only of God
& talks constantly of 'the future'.

loquitur puella

9

My loved one of recent nights
has gone. I consult
the diviners.
       Why does
the artless face
of a girl I
have never met
come to me in my dreams?

96

10

Conversations with a famous Lama,
queries about the eight-fold path
bring no conversion: What Lama
could deflect the thoughts that turn
again, again towards you?

11

In a season
        the shoots we planted
in last year's mud
        have become
handfuls of desiccated
        bent
fit for thatching.

In a season,
        the young men
have become stooped,
        their bodies curved
as the bent bows
        of the archers of Mu.

Who bends the bow?
Who loads youth with sudden age?

12

My third finger wears
        the signet ring
that closes
        secret business,
it is also a rifler
        of lips,
when a more formal
        present
is commonly looked for.

Egg-born ladies,
        do you keep
the top set
        close? Or
guilelessly reopen
        one
with t'other,
        the shared gift
with 'tasteful' *reportage?*

13

Three words at the market stall
and she & I have made
a knot
        of 'country matters'.
A knot so tied
no needle takes
but love-hours -days
or -weeks to loose
the impermanent ribbons.

14

The jade, Fortune
        tossed her head up
& whinnied.
        I took the reins in my hand.
I said: "Now,
        I'm in the saddle."

And straightway
        her Mother asks me
to dine,
        whose daughter I
play with
        nightly
in my dreams,
        nor because of her
am I content,
        nor can I read
or stay quiet
        in my own room.

15

She did not come
        from a woman
but out of a tracery
        of peach twigs
in bud,
        and love makes her fade
as sun & air
        make fade
silently, the peach flower.

16

The old dog
        at the west postern
has a yellow beard
        and is discreet
as the discreet Mandarin
        whom he resembles,
he does not betray
        my dusk departure
nor my return
        at dawn.

The Lion Throne
        stands empty,
the stiff ceremonial robes
        are hidden
in a clothes closet.
        Here,
I am the best drinking
        comrade,
the consoler
        of fifty young women.

Into the bedroom
        with the first light
comes snow light,
        we look out
and snow has filled the streets.

Though my good Mandarin
        opens but one eye
a black snow-snake
        clamours
from downtown Lhasa
        all the way
to the Potala walls.

17

I hold before my face
the Lama's holy face:
a blank appears.

I close my eyes,
my loved one is absent:
the unsensed lineaments grow
distinct, distinct
in the void.

18

On market days
        the dust-cloaked streets
of Lhasa
        throng with country people,
and those from Chung-gyel
        are by far
the handsomest.

Today I wait
        in a quiet corner
of the market
        for a goose-girl
with plump hips,
        who comes from Chung-gyel.

19

She passed me
        leaving a trail
of perfume
        to elaborate
my desire.
        I followed
through the streets.
        In a secluded alley
two strangers made
        unthinking love.
That done
        we parted.
I am the fool
        who found a coloured stone
that could be precious
        and threw it
(unthinkingly) away.

20

The ferry boat shoves off – heedlessly,
        though her horse
turns its head back & neighs,
        but the girl
standing at its head, she
        whose tent I
shared these recent nights, does
        not look back.
Does the widening stream
        cancel a
faithful or a faithless
        love meeting?

21

What has been said can be unsaid.
There is always an eraser. (Water
for ink, Time for the spoken word.)

But the half-formed, unwilled
projections of the mind, neither
aborted nor brought fully to light –

Son' i guidatori, questi!
the unknown charioteers.

22

Our professional rifler of sweets,
        the blue winged bee
accepts the passing of the petalled season.

And I, who also have nosed honey,
        must I regret
sweet love run dry &/or the withered petal?

23

In summer
        this reed-patch
tainted
        the lakeside water
& couched
        the tranquil young goose
that nested here.
        Now,

winter crackling
       coats
the separate stalks,
        the reflection
of those days
     is like
white coal,
       & the young goose
lacking fire & a mirror
        stands dejectedly
on the bank.

24

Living
with her
in whom
my heart
is lost,

groping
beneath
the sleep
of ocean,
searching
the sea-bed
for the
pearl self-
formed in
boyhood

25

The beautiful daughters
            of successful men,
having read Sappho,
            think of the red apple
in the orchard.
            They would hate
to remain 'on the shelf'
            but calculate
that looks that are o.k. anyhow
            can only be more so,
squirted with aromas
            of inaccessibility.

26

In the oasis of the day
            she is with me
but I cannot,
            for reasons of circumspection,
touch her small hand
            too often
or let my eyes
            too lovingly rest
on her amber skin.

When night returns
            and sleep is a mirage
hands
            fresh from her touch
flutter before my eyes,
            eyes
in which hers are reflected
            ogle
me from the darkness.

27

The looks I throw
        into the bunch of them
send ripples along
        their white teeth.
I give each
        separate attention,
but their smiles
        slide off my smiles –

And one,
        as I turn to her neighbour,
looks back at me
        from under the tail
of her false lashes
        with caution.

28

Walking in the gardens of her mind
and finding my own fears there
I look for a way back.
                        I ask her:
"What happens to love?
                        Can love live
beyond love's days?
                        Will our love live
afterwards?"
                She replies:
"Distance
        cannot part us in life,
how of time
        then in death?"

29

I look into your face.
        You show me
that you are smiling
        for you stretch
your lips back
        from your teeth.

I part your bodice.
        My right hand man-
handles your left breast.
        What is it
curled in the heart
        there... beneath?

30

Frost
        lacing
late summer
        grass
gives warning
        of autumn
winds.
        The honeyed
season
        is over.
The bee
        takes leave
of the flower.
        I
bow myself
        from your bed.

Poems 1968—1971

YOUNG LOVE IN OLD AGE

Young love in old age,
He must bury his dreams,
The timbers are creaking,
The old house is coming down,
She's on the town,
Life is as life seems.

Autumn flowers
Nipped in the bud,
There's frost in the yard
Where they buried the possum –
Made its love-nest
Under the boards
Near his lonesome bed.
The construction boys,
The bulldozers,
Did their bitter best,
Drove the whole family
In from next door.
This used lumber
Spits in the fire
Like green wood.
Green love in winter
Is nipped before flower.

This is the hour
The timbers creak,
The old house must come down,
She's split for good,
Life is as life seems,
He must bury his dreams.

HAND IN HAND IN THE PARK

Hand in hand in the park
Where dogs & children play
We stroll together
With few words to say.

Old folks sun themselves
Children play & chase,
We live each others' minutes
Stretched briefly face to face.

Hold my hand in yours
Let me touch your cheek
Kiss me while the blossom
In your hair smells sweet.

The dark will soon come down
Scoop shadows in your cheek,
Soon, soon will Time
Give Love his words to eat.

Kiss me while the blossom
In your hair still smells sweet,
The lights & loudness lessen
At the end of the street.

The park has vanished,
Quiet the town,
Only footsteps in your head
As the dark comes down.

What knocking at the door?
What night of storm & sleet?
What face no longer yours?
Who is there to meet?

What face no longer yours?
Who is she that's gone?
What face no longer yours?
Who is there to meet?
And who is she that's dead?

JUSTICE IS INVISIBLE

Justice is invisible,
    Law is bought & sold,
Love scuttles under the flesh
    For fear of taking cold.

What is there to see
    By day & talk about?
The madmen in the board rooms
    Compulsively shooting it out.

Justice is invisible
    And Love is blind,
What chance have we of catching
    The petal on the wind?

Neighbors are like us – I've heard,
    Law raps: "Love your brother."
Love is silent,
    She simply needs another.

Love needs him in the daytime,
    When all acts sleepwalkers are,
Not only at night
    Under Love's star.

Love come out of the flesh,
    Walk in the sun & wind,
Pluck the apples from the trees,
    Show you are not blind.

Love is all the life we've got
    So why complain?
Love is the neighbors,
    Frost & wind & rain.

When Love walks out & about
    In the taxi & the bus,
The tall buildings gossip:
    "There is no one but us."

Your head is crowned with towers
    That touch the prickly stars
Where apples, doves & sparrows
    And the rose that Love encloses
Strip bare the fearsome hours.

And what is there left beside
    Your can & my express,
Made just like our neighbors'
    To endure, more or less?

Love is all the life we've got
    So why complain?
Your weeping & my laughter
    And the wind & the rain.

THE HOMECOMING

They placed the Bow of Divination
in my left hand –
they helped me to bend it.

TWANG!
          I the Archer, I the Goal.
The arrow has buried itself at my feet.
Since that hour
one walks constantly at my side,
whom none see.

They have shut me behind glass.
They have shut me out from myself.
That I may look in on myself.
They have shut the doors on my soul.
I, ever the other I.

Pray, Masters:
          What Diviners must I visit?
What questions put?
How answer when, with all formality, they ask:
"And who, Great Lord, do you consider yourself to be?"

As needle between poles.
Steady. Hold steady.
Knowing that they will meet.
When the ice-flow breaks.
When the walls crumble.
When the prisons melt,
the barricades are torn down
and daylight & the open street
replace the nightmare & the dark wood.

At the hour of recognition.
Friendly. The homecoming.
This, our dwelling.

IS THE PRAYER

It is a sort of praying
listening
to the rain
down walls outside
falling
on leaves & flowers
a sort of praying
listening
accepting
as flowers the rain
praying
with no god listening
to the prayer
only you
who listens
to your own self
listening

is the prayer

Yes. Pushkin was
a colored man.
The word means
'little cannon'.
His granpa's vir-
ility was
astounding all
the women ran
after him after
which the poet
was (besides) a
man of honor,
so much so he
fought a duel he
didn't have to.
And got killed.
'Twas *Sturm und Drang*
all over again:
Schiller & Goethe &
The Byronic Hero.
Next comes Lermontov.

AUBADE

Love betwixt my love & I
In the thickets of Betune
All a Tuesday night did lie
While we played beneath the moon,
                    till the dawn breaks
& the big-mouthed lark awakes
Us, crying: "Lovers Away!"
And he would softly turn, say:
      "Sweet heart's delight
            Not dawn yet, not day,
      Runs still the night,
            That lark's crazy".

And then, then my love draws nigh
Yet not, not for me too soon
That can naught of love deny
But kiss for kiss, boon for boon
                    give what he takes,
Until the doubled heart so aches
Night a doomsday were we pray
So that he no more need say:
      "Sweet heart's delight
            Not dawn yet, not day,
      Runs still the night,
            That lark's crazy".

Anonymous, 12th century

The year steps out of winter
Wind & cold & rain
Into broidery again
Of sunlight fine & clear.

Nor beast nor bird is there
Whose tongue does not proclaim,
"The year steps out of winter
Of wind & cold & rain."

Fountain, burn, river,
In orfevreried train
Don links of silvered chain:

All, new clothes wear
When Spring steps out of Winter.

Charles d'Orléans

'MORT!'

I cry who laid his kiss
On my sweetheart's mouth
And will not slake his drouth
Until I too am his –
             Death!

Gone my manliness,
"What irked you in her youth,"
I cry, "to lay your kiss
On my sweetheart's mouth?"

Two that had one heart between us,
Gone the one, gone both.
In life sans Life / as Death alloweth
I, a gargoyle cry / hungered of this.

                   Villon

'DICTES MOY OÙ...'

Tell me where is *Flora*
Beautiful in Rome – where
Thaïs, Archipiada
Each as other fair,
Or, calling by still water
Echo, with her reply:
"My beauty is more than human."
Where are the snows goneby?

Where is worldly-wise *Elois*
Holding Abelard first
Her eunuch, then at St Denys
Her monk – by love accurst,
Or *Marjorie* of Burgundy
Commanding Buridan die
Dumped in a sack in Seine?
Where are the snows goneby?

White Queen *Blanche* whose
Voice was like the Sirens
Singing, *Berta Big-shoes,*
Alis, Bietris, Erembors,
The *Goosegirl of Lorraine*
The Goddams will fry –
Ask *God's Mother* where they've gone.
Where are the snows goneby?

ENVOI
No, reader, ask no more –
Today, tomorrow, where they lie
– The answer *Echoes* as before:
Where are the snows goneby?

Villon

'QUAND VOUS SEREZ BIEN VIEILLE...'

Helen by evening candlelight grown old
    Carding grey wool beside the hearth-fire blaze
    Shall, singing these words conjured in your praise,
Say: "Thus Ronsard my loveliness extol'd."

Of all the womenfolk in your household
    That nod, work-drowsed, by fire & candle rays
    None, but at my bruit, her quick head shall raise,
Blessing your name in words of hammered gold.

I shall be home to shades of underground,
My ghost at rest, 'mid dim-wreathed myrtles crowned;
    You, worn old woman, grieving by the grate

For my lost love that your fierce pride refused.
Pluck, pluck Life's Rose today, as Love is used:
    For Love – Life – Rose – tomorrow comes too late.

after Ronsard

Beata, come! The Rose
we watched at dawn unclose
her red robe to light
by nightfall has shed
fold, fold her robe of red
tints like lips bright.

Alas! The space is brief
the Rose holds the leaf.
Beauty falls away.
Stepdame Nature gives
flowers kindless lives –
a single day.

If then, Sweet, you would believe me
give not Age this chance to grieve thee.
Gather your Youth in its green hour,
while Love in sap is fixed in flower,
for you, like the Rose, its petals shed,
in time, by Time, shall be ravishèd.

Ronsard

from ASTAPOVO or What We Are To Do

TRADITION

for Gary H. Brown

I wish I was a Red Indian
    like Charlemagne,
I would take what I wanted
    because it was already mine.
I would cross the Rhine
    & eat up all the countries.

        The elephant horn
        still sounds
        among the chestnut
        woods in the pass
        at Roncesvaux.

And when I was old
    I would go to the wild prairies,
where the young buffaloes
    remain unharassed by the mating season.
They will acquaint me with the indifference of wild flowers.
I shall learn from Death what I did not learn from life.
And my children will pee in the white thickets of my beard.

IDENTITY

for Lucy Cohen

Rubble dust crumbling sand-
stone gives no grip to suede
brothel creepers while red
fat white rich ride by on
once wild burros whose hooves
effect clear trail tracks but
rich feet of fat lookers
never touch ground never
worry I said if you
cannot six months later
quote what you have just read
it will be simpler to
carry the book around
with you & turn to the
necessary page the
wayside notices a-
gainst cliff or top
of rainworn post offer
depth distance gone & to
go geological
strata thru which one is
rising or falling shards
etc of info angel
shale yields bed for numerous
sweet water springs in the
offing hence shrubs flowering
judas trees & the bent
& edible grasses
(three-quarters of the way
down ceased reading these signs)
said feeling the ef-
fect of your affective
nature on others you

shall cease to lie in bed
in the morning & in
the (FAD) supermarket
jammed in the pay gate at
the moment of arrest /
request / or if you like
truth agitating my
check folder & Blue Cross
Identification Card
yelled, "*I have my*
                    identity!"
Wind & water rounded
surface quartz moss agate
stone the matrices in
turquoise signal hiero-
glyphic affects of ALL &
even the Grand Canyon
is different because I
have gone down into it
carried you unknowing
                    along with me

FAD: Food At Discount

DISCRIMINATION

for John Elton

Nausicaa's girls
          the whole giggling gaggle of them
burrowing their bottoms in the sand, kneeling,
making little wheelbarrows of themselves,
lisping the tenderest obscenities,
the happiest girls in Phaeacia, each
with a good hard fuck for the wanderer.
Odysseus, alas! must discriminate.
Like all wanderers he knows it is the Princess or nothing.

Pound opined
          it was 'difficult to discriminate in America',
food, clothing, looks, honey & wine/being
OFFICIALLY HOMOGENEOUS.
                    On the golden Californian coast
I count one hundred-&-twenty Phaeacians
undergoing long-range acts of copulation
with the sun. I could contentedly masturbate
myself into each of those male/female bodies –
REVERSING HOMER.
                    The Homeric past shines on the shore,
destructible as life.

We all wish Odysseus had stayed longer
          the climate was clement –
snow does not lie long in Phaeacia.
          Homer liked that bit too:
the wanderer rehearses all that has happened,
          the minstrel's eyes glint through the mask.
The past shines in our knowing it.
          The past lives only in our knowledge of it.
Who but the poet can be our mediator?

On main lands
        snow empties
awkward things
        of awkwardnesses.
Snow makes void.
        And the Falcon hangs blindly in the void.
Among hollows that edge water
        smaller birds –
the pollen-gatherers
        – hop
happily
    the crocus & the daffodil between.
Flower-filled hollows that edge water
repel attentions of mindless snow.

Order is a convention of the blind.
When you feel like an octopus put your tentacles away.
When you feel like relating   : discriminate
When you feel like domesticating   : discriminate
When you feel like DOMINATING : discriminate

HOME

for Priscilla Minn

'Home is where you are'
And where you are is every place you've been.
I have so many homes
I lose myself when I stop to think about it
And I wonder will I ever come home?
Home is what you carry around with you.
Those who have no homes are at home all over.
Home is what you put under the pillow at night.
Home is behind love-curtain hair.
Home is under water.
Home is in the eyes & lips.
Home is inside.

Home is where you're never not,
Where hot is cold & cold is hot,
A Time & Place that love beguiles,
Where smiles are tears & tears are smiles.

The cat is in the kitchen sink,
Baby screams until it's pink,
Little sister, little brother
Curiously inspect each other.

Granma's crochet's caught on fire,
Mailman's bitten by desire,
Crochet's only for our betters,
Mailman's eating all the letters.

Daddy's yellen, on a bummer,
Fallen off the bough of summer,
Out of the apple-tree you float
With springtime in your eyes & throat.

Light in your eyes & dark hair
Telling the young wanderer
That Home like Love is all along
The eyes in which we both belong.

ROBIN HOOD / MAID MARION

for Christopher Logue

I cannot understand a woman
I want to make a woman the earth
or hill or moon or tree
I walk on the earth
& keep the sky above my head
this is how I make my poems

How do they make their poems? what poems?
it is important that they make their poems
what would it be like to be inside the earth
or moon or hill or tree?
are they inside & not inside?
they are not the earth. that's fable
bow-wow! they have to be earth to make my poems

I want to be Maid Marion, let her be Robin Hood
give me my antlers
the cuckold's an androgynous beast
bow-wow! cuck-a-riddle-doe!
when she unzips her skirt to fuck or frick
I leave the timber door a-crick

Cleft foot in the dappled wood
take her, John, enjoy the meal
I munch your Adam's Apple that she for me does steal
Robin is Maid Marion
Marion Robin Hood

134

IN THE PASS

for Bruno Dozzini

Mountain
      rain
blurs
      gun
sights
      thought
hardens
      will
flares
      as strength
lessens

Jungle tendril
      & rock-face
block the road

The cause was lost before we came to this valley

In the telescopic lens
      the militia boy
pees in his pantaloons
      with fear
he feels
      the bullet's climax
in the caress of the hair-trigger

The record in the diaries is only partial
Who will come in our tracks?

JOURNEY

for William Cookson

Between old & new moon
the bird flies in its shadow
between old & new moon
the swan sits on its reflection
between old & new moon
the harbor has vanished
between old & new moon
where is the wharf?
where are the vessels – the seamen?
between old & new moon
polarities are suspended
between old & new moon
the door that opens on yourself
typing in the next room
between old & new moon
there is no hunting
between old & new moon
eye claw talon
lack custom
between old & new moon
all rites are suspended
between old & new moon
the rite of passage

The dread encounter in the dark wood
as when some lighted window I pass by
shakes me with childhood dreams

And when the cage door flies wide
is it you blocking the doorframe?
as I pass that lighted window
are you seated in the room beside me?

136

LONELINESS

for Max Reese

I look at the wall in front
    the wall behind my head
stares back at me

all day old music plays
    sunlight has gone
the room seems wide & long

the newsman squawks
    in the parakeet's cage
the bird sings in the radio

chairs & tables
    lovingly arranged
walk out the door

I take my summer rose
    & place it (lovingly)
in the frigidaire freeze chest

what dreams the moon tonight
    in her lover's head?
what thoughts does she violate?

does she carefully prepare
    the supper
of fried mustaches?

I take my dentures out
    & lock them
in the piggy bank

my teeth & money
       are both safe
I fold my clothes

the vacant moonlight
       on the pretty pillow
opens her empty arms

VILLON ON DEATH

for Basil Bunting

POETRY TO GO
that's what
    Villon bought
at the hot dog
    stand
        the sleek hot dogs not so hot
        blotched thighs round a worn twat

Death. Margot
    sans linen
kept one wolf warm
    when the pack ran
through the streets
    outside her kitchen
in the cold season,
    I,
Francis Villon
    clerk, poet
who lived by
    the short dagger
hung
    mid-stomach
between shanks.
    No engine cranks
the restless tongue
    the nicked lip.
Montfaucon
    temporal exit
from the death pit.
    The last jack-off
free
    on the city

gibbet,
    the turnip topped
galvanic in death
    the jack-rabbit.

A THRU Z

for Sylvia Bruce

Everything gone!
Beneath the railing wind
naked as when born.
We have to begin
here as we have to end.
Strangle self-scorn
be fearful of pity.
Sight by Hell Fen's clear
as in Heaven's City.
Mirk half-light clings

to neither living nor dead.
Alone in this quiet room
words mysteriously move
out of somnambulance bred
of communion: the sole
life life brings.

from The Crystal Mountain

THE CRYSTAL MOUNTAIN

This alm hangs
    on the Crystal Mountain
where sky-cloud
    & valley-mist
her breath & mine
    meet
& become
    the shared place
like the wine
    from the white grape-
crop thin
    at this height
that permeates
    the walk's pause.

Sun rare
    soil-rock
trees less
    towards
the snowline
    upwards
no sound
    dark conifers
Dindymia's face
    the peaks
'with turrets crowned'

Here
    no Fountain
elixir
    nor common
Spring, not Heaven
    nor yet (quite)

Earth,
     but the wine
"Bitte Wein!"
     as lovelip to cup's lip
inclines
     mouth to brim
lip as smooth lip
     has kissed
he-her
     she-to-him
speaks of both.

EPIGRAM

The gnomon speaks not
but the stars
that faintly touch it.

Your heart
distant as starlight
speaks not,

But your body
at the shadow of Love's lightest approach
gossips freely.

SHRINE

Bugloss
mallow
& corn-
flower

breath-
ing fingers
early
plucked

placed here
(caged
sun-breath
'love
in submission'
till night &
petal
fall

Dead the petal
cold the hand
fled breath
devotion, dead

in quest,
the Moon
her shrine
reluming

death
subsumes.
Endymion
wakes.

SONG

The small bird sings
      through the willow tree,
the willow embraces
      the small bird.

Who sees the bird
      for the tree?
Or notes the tree
      for the birdsong
clothing it?

Hid each in the other's love:
Nailed the Falcon, tamed the Dove.

THE WELL

The window-box frames
flowers, window
the Bay, clouds
San Francisco, this room
my young wife who
kneels at the window

is tending the pansies hanging
out there against the wall
straggling over the box-sides,
tentacles framed by movie-shadow play
light & birds & air-dust, moss
(i.e. house walls).
the splashed-dyed wet petals
floppy after rain.

And on the silent wall
of mind forever shine
in neat rows
in dark earth
dank under cottage-stone
those others
the single petal dye-splashed
flower that glows
where sun comes not
or, straggling, comes
through crumpled skyline
of tree that harbors

whose sprawled branches are
arranging the small scythe-mown
plot of appled grass

whose boxed well
with winch for pail
plunges skywards
the child with it

who is kneeling
tending
the winch,
leaning
over the box-side,

whose face framed
by flowers of clouds
birds, leaves, etc.,

shatters,
where the bucket dips.

SESTINA

A girl? or an old man? which is the River?
whose the light that penetrates the Wood?
over what hidden valley stands the Hill
happily flowing into orchard, garden, Field
where kids & childing women in the farm-House
cut beast-masks under the hunting Moon?

The long-haired water blankens with the Moon
that washes now the boulders in the River
looping the orchard-trees beyond the House,
where day-sun-petal-fruit swirl past the Wood
whose leaning limbs under the red-edged Field
embrace in swimming the inverted Hill.

Daily in sunlit water hangs the Hill
nightly above whose summit swims the Moon
her vacant waters flooding the furrowed Field
where only boulders point to the drained River
that talks between the orchard & the Wood
darkly by night of day to the farm-House.

Expectant with parturition the farm-House
waits beside the orchard under the Hill
whose slopes upwards the palpitating Wood
mounts riddled with blind shafts of naked Moon
body that childs in burrow, spawns in River
& all else mads in byre, thicket, Field.

The valley floor looks one divided Field –
scrub, farrow, pasture & the human House,
the orchard next the red bank by the River
that slits the landscape through from hill to Hill,
amber & green in sun, blanked by the Moon,
– ringed with pinnacles of the hanging Wood.

With wildwood animals she stalks the Wood,
holding the hare transfixed in furrowed Field
Hecat, Lucina & Dian, the Moon
has entered the child's mask, drawn birth to House,
in triune power flooded valley & Hill,
wedded boulder, subsumed the girlish River.

THEIRS where burrowed Wood falls to furrowed Field
where River still runs close under the Hill
for beast & man THE HOUSE-MASKS OF THE MOON.

The Genealogy of Women

adapted from Semonides of Amorgos

THE GENEALOGY OF WOMEN

God in His Wisdom from the start
Set Man & Woman poles apart,
And out of Woman's nature drew
A veritable human zoo.

   The slattern s o w 'mid pans & pots
& unwashed clothes & garbage squats,
Her very skin as thick with dirt
As are her stockings, shirt & skirt –
Maid of middens that still battens
On household waste – and fat, fattens.

   Maliciously, the long-nosed VIXEN
Of Good & Bad won't choose betwixt 'em.
Restless, till the heart of rose
Smells like a cabbage – cabbage, rose –
Exudes the stench of human stews
Dressed as the kindliest piece of news.

   Next, the BITCH, whose business is
Everyone else's businesses.
Inquisitive, like the she-fox,
With eye at keyholes, ear at locks,
Nosing for what her neighbor knows,
Yapping the secret to disclose
(Or when there's nothing to disclose).
Threats, blows on the mouth, a kind word,
She stays oblivious as a turd.
Set her where discretion matters,
As host or guest – still she chatters.

   The fourth, SEA, a schizophrenic,
Floods with manners quite Hellenic,
Laughter & wine, etcetera,

The guests, who do not find bizarre
The rapid talk, seductive glance,
But find themselves bewitched – entranced...
In unison they dumbly bray
Their compliments, nor do they say
Aught of her manners the next day,
Her husband's private perquisite.
From room to room, from fit to fit,
She snaps like her own bitch at bay
Keeping some puppy thieves away.
You cannot look, you may not touch –
To friends & enemies she's such.
And such is sea – in summer, calm,
That sailors there nor dream not harm;
But winter comes when seas in clouds
Shall bomblike burst on masts & shrouds,
Whence Tars, like Husbands, drown in crowds.

    The ASS, proverbially stubborn,
Must be doubly so in Woman.
Of what avail the goad & lash,
Threats, carrots, kindness, even cash?
Little performed & less achieved –
Who, losing her, could feel bereaved?
Two things she does: she eats & swives,
Enough for half a hundred wives.
She'll eat you out of house & home
And swive her way through half of Rome.

    Of all the sounds of English, 'CAT'
Can never justly rhyme with 'twat',
And yet the two together go
As all who've eaten pussy know.
The CAT hunts with her sexual part
Directed at some bed-mate's heart,
Whose appetite is rudely quenched,
Who cries, "Never shall I be wenched

"Like that again. My stomach's sick.
"You make kind love a dirty *trick*."
Scrounger, CAT, of others' lovers,
Who licks friends' plates for leftovers.

    As is well known, the Sexual Tease
Will seldom do it on her knees,
For Women then have less control
Of the performance as a whole.
The well-bred delicate FILLY
Acts like this – her sex-tastes chilly.
She likes to stir, likes to arouse
But finds it odious to douse.
If fuck she must, then fuck she will,
But he will go unsated still.
To sate that vice that feeds on vice
A thousand times will scarce suffice,
And in a thousand copulations,
With all their various permutations,
Something goes of that precious 'me',
Whose full submersion is the fee
Love takes of Woman as bed-mate
Who duly would her partner sate.
But little as she cares to fuck,
Less cares she to clean out muck.
Less to sit beside the oven
Raking ash like any sloven.
The labor she delights in still
Is that in which she has most skill:
To comb, to cream, to scent, to dress
Her hair, her skin, her limbs, – caress
With fair hands so fair a body
Other bodies look just shoddy.
An object, she, to be displayed
Like some old useless piece of jade
Commercially by men in trade
Whose pride it is to own & show;

159

All other men must she bring low.

The ugly APE, as worst of all
Should have been listed first of all.
Lacking Eve's tender flesh & bone
She seems more like some mouldy stone.
A square head set on square shoulders,
Like those prehistoric boulders
That in shape look vaguely human,
Such is this misshapen woman.
A sort of anthropomorphic clown
That moves 'mid mock'ry through the town.
And like some clowns, and like all APES
With spite she spikes her witless japes,
Heeds not the neighbors' just derision,
Thrives on malice & misprision.

And last, the humble bumble BEE
That I & Meleagro (he
Who started the Greek Anthology)
And also Rgya Mts'o, sang
(Whose other names were Ts'angs & Dbyangs) –
The BEE in this brute list arrives,
And here we find the best of wives.
What honey would you rather eat
Than that she spins from Love's sweet seat?
What distillation ever comes
More dear than from her honeycombs?
Women, 'tis known, swap tales of Love,
This woman's life of Love is wove:
She has no time for Love's tit-bits
But spews out honey where she sits.
Daily about her wifely chores,
Eager to earn her man's applause.
By night she stills his rightful lust,
By day she mops the household dust.
A happy, useful life, you think,

Spent beside the kitchen-sink?
'Tis true, yet let no man forget,
There comes a time when Love shall set.
And she'll call in her woman's debt.
Love in its fullness like a peach
She'll then accept from each & each.
For this Queen BEE – 'tis known to all –
Consumes her lovers in the Fall.

Although Man runs to take a wife
She works him mischief all his life.
The even tenour of a day,
The sense that debt is kept at bay,
To all of this he'll kiss goodbye.
And when he thinks he's hit a high,
That God is pleased with him, or Man,
And he has done the best he can,
That's when his wife in ambush waits
Slamming Euphoria's happy gates
With words relentless as the Fates'.
He asks his friends: she makes a scene;
Or, if she would appear serene,
Then's when the poison works the worst,
Then's when she's well & truly curst.
And all the while his wife is *his*;
Others, potential mistresses.
He praises her; the others mocks,
And does not see the paradox.

Of all the woes God's given Man,
Woman, especially Woman's can(–)
Can honestly be said to take
The torta, tart, or bun, or cake.
The sexual drive in Man or Woman
Is all the sexes have in common.
In Man, the sex & love are one,
In her, this union is undone.

From this divorce derives that pain
The whore lays on with whip & cane.
All ills, desires, fruitless prayers,
Discords, empty acts & wars
Are in those eyes, those thighs, that hair
That ride Man's sexual despair.

And who among us now, a boy,
Could carelessly set sail for Troy?
For Helen's gestures, walk, her glance,
More deadly than the haft of lance
That entered once her erstwhile friends,
For us no deathless cause portend –
Merely the *pettiest* of ends.

Is there no other path to tread
Than that of the Achaean dead?

Seven from The Greek Anthology

1

'Drink to me only...' – BEN JONSON

It is not wine that makes me reel
    Not juice of grape I crave,
Only to drink where you have drunk
    A wine no grape e'er gave.

Let but your lip the wine-cup lip
    Touch – how can I flee
Or wine, or sweet cup-bearer, for
    The kiss it bears of thee?

Agathias

2

You expect, Puss-in-Boots
    to go on treating my house
as your house
    after treating my pet partridge
as a comestible?

    No, pet partridge!
Over the bones of his treat
    the cat shall be slain,
& you honoured in blood rite:
    As Pyrrhus, recall,
(rightfully) slew
    Polyxena
over the corpse of Achilles.

Agathias

3

Epitaph in the Borghese Gardens

Powder-light let dust lie
On Musa, who had blue eyes,
Who made bird-sweet music,
That all heard, all praised,
Who, silent now, stone-still,
     Here lies.

Anonymous

4

Lacking rich acres, thick grape-crops
Old Euphron, his plough as old as he,
Scrapes share-cropper's soil –
Grape-harvest thin, hard found:
First-fruit gifts ever meagre.
But let the year's crop swell,
Shall not the god's tithes too increase?

Apollonides

5

Beeman Cliton hews
From the flower-fed hive
Sweet honey-crop, Spring's
Gift, ambrosial, pressed
From combs of his far-
Roving flock... Let but his
Multitude of singing bees
Fill full with honeyed wine
Their wax-built cells.

Apollonides

6

Snow, clothing sky & mountain,
Drives the shy, pointed deer
To valley river, whose moisture
Still is warm. Improvident frost
Chains them there in painful ice.
Villagers, without fishing gear,
Catch what escaped the hunter's snare.

Apollonides

7

The cup clinks out, my friend
Diodorus, 'Sleep apes but Death'.
Wine! Here is wine. No water add,
But drink till your knees sag.
Soon, too soon, will come the day
When we no more shall drink
Together. Rouse up, Diodorus!
Age, sobriety, have touched our brows.

Apollonides

The Feast and The Gypsies

for Livia and Sabina

BLACKBERRY, BLACKBERRY

for Frances

Blackberry, blackberry
    Blue inside,
White cherry, white cherry
    I'm a bride,
Red berry, red berry
    Michael*mas*,
April Fool –
    And you're an Ass!

OUR HOUSE

Our house has a willow tree,
    Our house has a pond,
Our house has a kitchen garden
    With woods beyond.

Our house has fields,
    Our house has a hill,
Our house has fir trees
    Dark & still.

Two flat roads like a 'T'
    Divide our ground,
Barns, maple, lilac
    Jumbled all around.

Mummy's in the kitchen,
    Daddy by the stream
Teasing the fishes
    From their fishy dream.

Uncle Peter's in the garden
    Digging up the weeds,
Raking the furrow
    For the lettuce seeds.

Ducks rise from water,
    Cows graze in meadow,
Birds under the sun
    Chase each other's shadow.

Livia & Sabina
    Crouching side by side
In the island in the driveway
    Where we like to hide.

This is how it is
        In this house of ours
Where me & my family
        Spend our happy hours.

STILL LIFE

Gentle fawn in marble sleep,
        Cloven hoof to veinèd eye,
Orion lurks beyond the steep,
        Outside, a-cold, thy brethren lie.

Inside, upon the mantelshelf
        The clock, the mug, the pictures keep
Insentient vigil with thyself:
        The house is hushed in sleep... in sleep.

This afternoon the leaves like snow
        Silently fell about my head,
Snow fell with dusk and lieth now
        Beneath the snowlike moon outspread.

A-swoon beneath white forest boughs,
        Entranced beneath the moon's cold eye,
Across the fields, within the house,
        In swoon of sleep scarce breathing lie

Thy gentle brethren, gentle fawn,
        Locked fast in sleep as thou in stone
Until the dream-dispelling morn
        Insist the charming moon begone.

GATHERING WATERCRESS

Two figures by the snow-lipped stream
Stooped over, scooped out the stream's green hair,
Hair spread flat out, not moving in the hurrying water.
Mama said: *"Fetch me large-leafed messes*
For our salad-bowl today, of watercresses."
Back through brown woodscape they raced
Laughing, unaware
That that black water
Had swallowed (in exchange for hair)
Their two images,
Fixed now in the snowy wood,
Known to no comers else
But sunshine, rain, snow.

HAIKU

This caterpillar
whose furred coat has bark age-rings,
leaves in autumn fly.

BEE & FLOWER

The nymph
      in the mallow-flower
nods
      at the altar:

A blue-winged bee
      bangs
at the abbot's window.

THE THREE-LEGGED DOG

Along the road where the two farms stand
And where, half-fearful, you take my hand,
The three-legged dog makes an angry fuss
But it's not, my dear, that he's angry with *us*.
It's only the poor thing's confused – ashamed
Of having three legs – afraid he'll be blamed
For not being able (now that he's maimed)
To keep the old farm from two-legged thieves,
And the four-legged sort from the barley sheaves;
So he chases & barks & sets up a racket
To show that, though minus one leg, he can hack it.
Love the old dog then – you'd just as well,
For you know what 'dog' running backwards will spell.

FIRST RIDDLE

I am ship
I am book
I am house

Yoke sky to earth
Beast's friend, bird's & man's

Refuge in storms
Refuge in summer heats

Lightning I fear,
Fire & iron

Who am I?

SECOND RIDDLE

I gather myself in the tops of tall trees
I fold myself over fields & streets
I am soft & black
But you cannot stroke my 'fur'
Though you wish you could
And almost feel you might.

I am the divider
I am the consoler
To the wise I bring visions

To the foolish, fears,
Shadows are my children
Sleep, death, my companions.

I have as many eyes
As stars hang in the sky.

Who am I?

THIRD RIDDLE

Cherry I am not
Nor any fruit
Though I go by the names of many.

I have no color
Though colors issue
Coldly from me.

Dancers
Frenetic stick-players
Mammoths
Are in my power.

I give much pleasure on long summer afternoons.

Dead fish know me.

As does Judas Iscariot.

Who am I?

FOURTH RIDDLE

I am in this body
Which is in this chair
Which is in this room
Which is in this house
And body chair room house are among these trees

Which are in this wood
Which is on this hill
Which is part of earth
And wood hill earth are part of this world

Which goes round the sun
Which is in the sky
Which is in the universe
And sun sky universe are in God's head

Which has universe
Which has sky
Which has sun
Which has world
Which has earth
Which has hill
Which has wood
Which has trees
Which has house
Which has room
Which has chair
Which has body
Which has me
In it

Who am I?

THE FEAST & THE GYPSIES

The butcher, the baker, the candlestick-maker,
The barber, the farmer, the priest
Have met in the square
And are offering there
An extraordinarily succulent feast.

There is candyfloss pie, a free-for-all fry
With bangers & toad-in-the-hole,
There are liquorice whips
With *green* chocolate chips,
Triple B's* & a vast tootsie roll.

The jolly fat mayor will loudly declare
"The feast has officially begun,
"Set-to with a will
"Chew, swallow & swill
"And remember that Fatness is Fun.

"A sweet Mary Jane on the end of a chain
"With M & M's, ketchup & beer
"Will go as a prize
"To the virtuous wise
"Who can eat more than anyone here."

And what a delight to be sure was the sight
Of goodies so greedily eaten,
Nor yet was one cent
By anyone spent
Until it was shown he'd been beaten.

For when the fat mayor (loved by everyone there)
Had finished his nine hundredth bun,

It was jointly announced
He roundly had trounced
All others – in fact he had won!

The cost of the feast, by him who'd had least
Was borne more than by anyone there,
While those who'd had most
Bore less of the cost,
As agreed upon there at the Fair.

It may not seem odd to you, me, or God
But always it seems to be so,
That less shall breed less
And more shall breed more
Wherever by ill-chance you go.

Yet outside the village, beyond Church & tillage
Are Gypsies, who dance round their fire,
Eat crab-apples raw
And know naught of the law
That fuels the flames of desire.

Not rich & not poor, on the crab-apple moor
With a wisdom all of their own,
Their humility may
Well have something to say
When the rats shall their rat-race disown.

* Bud's Butter Brickle, from Bud's Ice Cream at 24th and Castro,
San Francisco

THE MEETING

Tom the Miller's boy is there
At the hedgerow spring.
I run & fetch my bucket,
I join him at the spring.

The two pails clatter,
The west wind blows,
Broken bits of sunlight
In our pails dance in rows.

Black out of the spring
The water rushes,
It splashes in the bucket,
White where it flows –

White as the Miller's apron
White as my rose.

Two hands holding
The slip-slop bucket
Slow, slow
Up the road we go.

We put the buckets down
When we reach my door.
It is windy sunshine weather,
And he goes on up the hill
As so many times before.

I do not step inside
But where he goes, I stare.

The wind blows hard against me.

It whirls the rose out of my hair.

CAT & OWL

If the cat
Ate the bat
And sat
On the fireside mat
Afterward,

Licking her fur
By the fire
Every purr-purr
A purr of filled desire,

What would the bird
Who had heard
Every, every word
But not stirred

From its perch
In the church-
Tower's belfry
Say? –
          "Nay, nay"?
"No way, no way"?

If 'twas the *owl*
On the prowl
Cruel as the cat,
No doubt that that
Bird's word
Echoingly heard
Around the house,
Loud but unseen
Across the green
By cat, rabbit, stoat, mouse

Would say –
"Yea, yea, yea
           yea, YEA."

NOBODY

When I awoke this morning
Nobody fled from my side,
He paused at the window
And then –
                    ran off to the woods to hide.

But although I followed him out
He would not let me play,
But wrapped himself round
With a wisp of the dawn
And floated away... away...

THE DAY THROUGH

Sunlight bright on
    Nursery walls,
"Get dressed, Livia,
    Morning calls."

Snowdrop, crocus
    Daffodil
Nod & dance while
    You sleep still.

There's leaves to rake,
    Beds to clean
Before summer's
    Shower of green.

Green the grass then,
    Green the trees,
Green the dreams we
    Have of these.

Now's the time to
    Make all ready,
Garden & House
    Fit for a Lady.

Up, to work
    With rake & hoe,
Broom, duster
    The day through.

And when dusk comes,
    Inside to eat,
With tousled hair,
    Tired feet.

Riddles & games
By the fireside,
'Snakes & Ladders',
'Guess the Bride'.

Firelight, starlight
Sleepy head,
"Upstairs, Livia,
Into bed."

THE HOUSE IS A HOME

The sunlight lingers longest in the attic,
The dusty playroom where others do not come.
The rays are filled with motes that dance away.
You cannot see them when the sun's not there.
The roof slopes so steeply you can stand upright
In the middle only, & just on either side.

The *salotto* takes the fuller, daytime sun
From ten to five or six o'clock, depending.
The sofa & chairs have flowered covers, the long drapes
      many folds.
Here are pictures, mirror, books & the piano
Its lid propped open. Often its notes sound out
Across the room where we all like to be.

The breakfast room the sun strikes first,
A clearer, cleaner light than in the attic later.
There are pots of marmalade & jam & honey
Butter, toast, *croissants*, with coffee milk.
The table's dark surface reflects your hands & food.

The kitchen floor is stone; windows are low & leaded.
There is a marble slab for drinks & cold foods.
Copper pans, iron kettles, hang beside the stove.
Herbs, flour & sugar are on closet shelves.
Onions & peppers, bacon, stretch from the ceiling.
Here is where snacks are eaten late at night,
Rich-smelling roasts & frothy stews prepared,
Plump pheasants & tawny rabbits plucked & skinned.

Served is this kitchen by its own garden
With tall sweet pea, vegetables in rows,
Raspberries, gooseberries, all that the season brings.

Upstairs, the windows are overhung by deep eaves.
Ivy & virginia creeper keep the house warm.
Most bedrooms have the sun come in at morning.
Others, the evening sun, when daytime's nearly over,
When it's time to go upstairs, undress, prepare for sleep.

The house knows us, it seems, and we the house.
It would not be a home without our love for it,
Nor we, ourselves, without its rootedness.

Boy
Girl
Toy
Curl
Love
Fancy
Dove
Nancy
Lip
Sip
Neck
Peck
Sashes
Lust
Dust
Ashes
Room
Womb
Doom
Tomb

(There are times
In English Rhymes
When Peaches & Cream
Are not all that they seem.)

Poems 1972—1982

THE SHADOW ON THE BLIND

The night my conspirator,
we watch her shadow
cast on the cottage blind
while she undresses.

The form is blurred
by muslin curtains
drawn before the blind.

Wrinkled in repose,
when the figure moves
it ripples.

Homeward then
down high-hedged lanes
the cottage light now hidden.

*   *   *

What Joy from love is cast!
What bright spring strength
Though blurred the blossom's end!
How happy Love in what is cast awry!
How Time, clasping the Rose, sends tremors through
        Love's body!
Not to be tainted, not to be despoiled,
Such Joy in Love must be!

A Joy that casts no shadow.

A SILVER BIRCH TREE IS MY LOVE

If dead I were to stretch myself
In these brown woods
Beside this lonely birch tree
There would be affinity between us.

As winter leaves, candied in ice
My still body, fingers etc.
Would accede to winter's goings-on.

I should not be lonely any more
As the birch tree is not lonely,
Nor should I see the Moon
As the birch tree certainly doesn't.
But the wind would rummage over me
As it does the tree
And it would not be bitter.

If I did not exactly put out roots
I should be of some help in the neighborhood:
Squirrels would find bits of my clothes useful.

Silver Birch!
Lonely & lovely among indifferent scrub,
Not less white than the snow that idles about us both.

What is the significance you hold for me?
Why should I fear it to be a cheat?
Fearful of not discerning truth of an affection.

Are affinities such as ours discernible
Only outside ourselves,
In actions or things we make
Such as this poem?
And how do our bodies enter into it?

I cannot nourish you,
Your skin is yours not mine,
My feet do not stick down into the earth,
And I can see the Moon.
The Moon in her phases makes me
Part of what I love.
What I love is my Paradise.
Bring me to my Paradise, Moon.
Close my eyes in Moonless night.
Lay me where fingers will not distinguish
Skin mine & not mine.
Lay me where the bitter wind
Opening my heart
Will seem less bitter
Than the coldness now inside.
Unlock my nature
That what I love may at last be wholly me.

Hillsdale,
New York, 1972

MEIN BLAUES KLAVIER

At home a blue piano stands,
No note of music do I know.

From cellar door the shadows spread
Since the world decayed below.

Duets played by four starred hands
– Moon-woman sings, boats row –
Now rats fandango on the keys.

The keyboard is unstrung, I shed
Tears that for the blue dead flow.

In life, dear Angel, open please
– I've bitten bitter bread of woe –
The doors of Heaven overhead,
Though through them yet I may not go.

Else Lasker-Schüler

COLLOQUE SENTIMENTAL

In the old, desolate park, in frost,
Just now two shapes walked past.

Their eyes deadened, their lips flaccid,
Their talk hard to catch.

In the old, desolate park, in frost,
Two shades call back the past.

"Remember that past ecstasy?"
"You want me to remember – why?"

"Your heart throbs at my name as ever?
My soul as ever comes in dreams?" – "Never."

"Days rare, of unspeakable bliss,
Lip kept to lip!" – "Doubtless."

"Heavens so blue and hope so high!"
"Hope took off, broken, into a black sky."

So through the long grass they walked,
Their talk only the night has caught.

Paul Verlaine

'COMME ON VOIT SUR LA BRANCHE...'

When on the branch in May the rose we view
Its springing freshness, its sweet flow'ring prime
Shaming the heavens with such living hue
As tears of daybreak wash at morning time,

Grace in the leaf and love reposing there
Odor of rose the trees & gardens holding
Till worn by rain, worn by the sun-drenched air
Languishing it dies, leaf on leaf unfolding,

So you, in flush, in newness of the rose
When earth & sky mere mirrors of you were
Has Fate killed cold, cold ashes you repose;
Take then each sigh, as obsequies, each tear,

Full flask of milk, frail* full of flowers – MARIE
Living or dead shalt thou but roses be.

Ronsard

* frail: pannier

196

'QUAND VOUS SEREZ BIEN VIEILLE...'

It is evening.
   You are old.
      My love is old.
Old are the words you sing.

My praise in mind
   among your maids
      at the loom,
"These words extol'd my bright looks."

The thread unravels.
   Fire sinks in the grate.
      The least of your maids' hair
gleams brightly.

The hour is late.
   Before your own disdain
      you sit
keening his love

Even as you sing
   the words therefrom.
      The room encloses
naught – of wine, of milk, of roses.

"Ronsard praised me so
All might my beauty know."

Pierre long gone *'mid shades of underground,*
A boneless ghost with dim-wreathed myrtles crowned.

Your roses crudded like love's milk unsucked,
Sour as wine the gods did not accept.

Pretty flower you would not pluck
Shrivelled e'er its hour has struck.

after Ronsard

'*JE VEUX LIRE EN TROIS JOURS L'ILIADE...*'

'*Shut, shut the door, good John...*'
— POPE: EPISTLE TO DR ARBUTHNOT

Give me my Homer
                    (if through Pope)
alone. Three days lock out
the outside world,
                    good John —
"Tie up the knocker!"
And, if slipped a dollar
you let slip some lout
to vex me with my Pope, my Homer
you'll feel the weight of a master's collar!

Not Dorothy, the chambermaid
who comes to make my bed with you,
not you yourself, good John,
to fix the room, my food —
three days of solitude
with Homer (if through Pope) I seek
then drunkenness for one full week.

If from Olympus one should – cleaving
the aether with winged feet –
descend on me, inform him, pray,
Homer & Pope & I
                       are weaving
our immortality.
               You may
keep the god waiting in the street.
Announce three days delay.

But if some messenger from her should call
scoop him at once within the hall.
Or she herself! Then, John, throw wide
my chamber doors that she may step inside
my arms.
           Shipwreck upon her bosom shall seem sweet –
plunged deep as lies the entire Homeric fleet!

after Ronsard

MA DAME, MA DOUCE PROVENCE

Ab l'alen tir vas me l'air
qu'eu sen venir de Proensa.

To breathe the air
of fair Provence
my thought makes dance
that men I hear
from there who say
her praise I pray
one hundredfold
for each word told –
and the heart smiles.

Not otherwhere
than 'twixt Durance
Rhône river, Vence
the sea, shines there
such bright joy day
where fine lust may
'mid peers behold
she whom I hold
all care beguiles.

Days thought on her
in whom & whence
all joys commence
no ill can bear,
true lauds gainsay
the praise men pay:
her looks of gold
cannot be told –
her world of wiles.

All that is rare
in the *gay science*,
that I enhance,
reverts to her
whose limbs lien lay
to all that I say,
all I've been bold
(as mine) to unfold –
witless the whiles!

after Peire Vidal

COPA

for Peter Jay

Syrian *barmaid with the* Greek *headscarf,*
    drunken & sexy in the dusky tavern
shaking her hips to the castanets,
    the raucous reeds at her elbows:

"Stuffed with summer dust outside?
    Rest-up on our drinking bench.
We've wine by the basin, goblet, ladle –
    flowers, flutes, fiddles – a patio cool with reeds.
Under *Arcadian* trellis *Pan's Pipes*
    trill sweetly in the shepherd's mouth.
Thin wine fresh from pitched amphora,
    water clattering in the creek-bed.
There's saffron stock in bunches,
    bunches of roses – crimson, gold,
& water-lilies washed by virginal
    water – *Achelois* in sacks of sedge.
Our small cheeses drain in rush containers.
    We've wax-like plums of autumn days.
Chestnuts too... the pippin blandly ripening.
    All held under *Ceres*... under *Cupid*... under *Bacchus.*
Here, thick grape-clusters, scarlet mulberries,
    the bluish melon from its stalk depending,
our cottage *Priapus* wielding his willow hook –
    no terror he, despite his outsize member.
Cybele's galla – priest! Your worn mule sweats.
    Pity your mule... mules, precious to *Vesta.*
The cicada's song bursts in the bushes.
    The speckled lizard lurks in his lair.
Wise, reclining, refresh in a summer's
    bowl yourself – or in calyxed crystal.

Under the vine-leaf's shade, take rest,
    that roses twine your tired temples,
that some marshmallow mouth be yours to nibble.

    "Archaic eyebrows – off!
Shall ingrate ashes smell the flowers we give?
    Would'st crown with them thy bones' tombstone?
Wine! Dice! There's no 'next'. *Death* tweaks your ear.
'Life's for living,' *Death* says, 'I'm here'."

                                        attributed to Virgil

HORTORUM DEUS

both for Bob Zachary

I

Youngsters! I,
          chopped roughly from dried oak-stump
protect this peat croft thatched with withies,
swathes of sedge.
                    Year by year it prospers.
Father & son, peasants both, tend me as their deity,
owners of this modest cottage.
                              One, with scrupulous care
cures my sanctuary of brake & briar,
t'other, with open hand yields
successively their small gifts.
On me they hang the first bright coronal of painted spring:
soft the virid blade, tender the ear of corn.
Mine, golden gillyflower & orange poppy,
pale marrow & sweet-smelling quince,
the flushed grape that dangles
from trained vine-tendril's shade.
Not seldom – not a word! – my altar-shrine
runs smirched with blood of bearded male,
of horn-hoofed female, goat.
                        For these devotions
Priapus protects their garden patch, their vineyard.
Ill-rifling, boys, reject. Be someplace else.
The next-door neighbor's rich; his Priapus idle.
Fill-up on him: this path will take you there.

attributed to Catullus

204

II

I, putative pilferer, I
with folk-craft fashioned
lo! from withered poplar
I, this leftward patch you see,
cot & plot of modest folk, keep free –
its quinces keep from pilfering fingers.
Mine, the polycolored buds of spring.
Mine, the copper corn of fervid summer.
Mine, the verdant tendrils of the swollen grape.
Mine, the grey-green olive of hard winter.
From my grazings, the delicate nanny
drags her milk-filled dugs to market.
From my folds, the well-fed lamb
remits a heavy fistful home.
Followed by its mother's *moos*, the tender calf
sheds its blood on altar steps.
Esteem this god therefore.
Pilfering hands hold-off –
on pain of penalty from a ready penis.
A 'pain' to cherish? The farmer comes. Watch
him unscrew the part you want, with fierce arm
raise the dexterous shillelagh.

attributed to Catullus

A QUESTION

Is the shadow
    of this bamboo shoot
that falls between us
    less real
than sun or leaf
    that casts it?

Are your eyes
    less real
in my eyes
    reflected
than in themselves?

Can flesh, eye
    bamboo stalk
ever themselves know,
    save Love
its looking-glass provide?

SELECT BIBLIOGRAPHY

POETRY

Clear Lake Comes from Enjoyment (Neville Spearman, London, 1959) with Denis Goacher
The Ingathering of Love (Work in Progress, Santa Barbara, 1967)
The Blue Winged Bee (Anvil Press Poetry, London, 1969)
ASTAPOVO or What We Are To Do (Anvil Press Poetry, London, 1970)
The Crystal Mountain (Sand Dollar, Berkeley, 1970)

VERSE TRANSLATIONS

The Marriage Rite (The Ditchling Press, Sussex, 1960) with Denis Goacher
Umberto Mastroianni: *The Detail and The Design* (Edizione Segnacolo, Bologna, 1962) with Mary de Rachewiltz
The Poems of Catullus (Penguin Classics, London and Baltimore, 1966; University of California Press, Berkeley, 1969)
The Poems of Meleager (Anvil Press Poetry, London, and University of California Press, Berkeley, 1975) with Peter Jay
Letter to Juvenal: epigrams from Martial (Anvil Press Poetry, London, 1984)

PROSE TRANSLATIONS

Boris de Rachewiltz: *Black Eros* (Allen & Unwin, London, and Lyle Stuart, New York, 1964)
Boris de Rachewiltz: *Introduction to African Art* (John Murray, London, and New American Library, New York, 1966)

INDEX OF TITLES

For the untitled poems of *Love Poems of the VIth Dalai Lama* and the versions from *The Greek Anthology,* the first line is given.

DATE DUE

#47-0108 Peel Off Pressure Sensitive